STUDY ABROAD

How to Get the Most Out of Your Experience

Michele-Marie Dowell
Hampden-Sydney College

Kelly P. Mirsky
Illinois State University

Prentice
Hall

Library of Congress Catagloging-in-Publication Data

Dowell, Michele-Marie.
    Study abroad: how to get the most out of your experience / Michele-Marie Dowell,
Kelly P. Mirsky.
        p. cm.
    ISBN 0-13-049997-8 (paper adhesive)
    1. Foreign study——Handbooks, manuals, etc. 2. American students——Foreign
countries——Handbooks, manuals, etc. 3. International education——Handbooks, manuals,
etc. 1. Mirsky, Kelly P. II. Title

    LB2376 .B69 2003
    378'.016——dc21

                                                                              2002032378

Publisher: Phil Miller
Sr. Acquisitions Editor: Bob Hemmer
Asst. Director of Production: Mary Rottino
Editorial and Production Supervision: Kelly Mulligan/Carlisle Publishers Services
Asst. Prepress and Manufacturing Manager: Mary Ann Gloriande
Prepress and Manufacturing Buyer: Brian Mackey
Cover Design: Kiwi Design
Editorial Assistants: Meghan Barnes, Peter Ramsey

© 2003 by Pearson Education, Inc.
Upper Saddle River, New Jersey 07458

Printed in the United States of America

ISBN 0-13-049997-8

Pearson Education LTD., London
Pearson Education Australia PTY, Limited, Sydney
Pearson Education Singapore, Pte. Ltd.
Pearson Education North Asia Ltd., Hong Kong
Pearson Education Canada, Ltd., Toronto
Pearson Educación de Mexico, S. A. de C. V.
Pearson Education - Japan, Tokyo
Pearson Education Malaysia, Pte. Ltd.
Pearson Education, Upper Saddle River, New Jersey

CONTENTS

ON-SITE

RE-ENTRY

APPENDICES

PREFACE

PREFACE TO THE PROGRAM ADMINISTRATOR

As a professional educator involved in a study abroad program, you probably already offer your students an orientation for their experience abroad. But if you are like us, you are often left feeling that you wish you could share so much more with your students. By the time you complete the "required" components of getting students abroad, there is often little time to devote to more advanced discussions about cross-cultural understanding, overseas adjustment, and profound personal growth.

Currently, most study abroad programs have expanded orientation sessions to include not only the do's and don'ts and other specific programmatic information but also extensive question-and-answer sessions—often with past participants being present to give the "student perspective." We may even include cross-cultural simulation activities designed to get the students thinking about how they may feel once abroad.

But no matter how we structure the predeparture orientation, we are confronted with a set of built-in limitations. First, students are inundated with information in these sessions and often walk away overwhelmed. It's difficult to avoid the pitfall of information overload as we try to share wisdom about this upcoming event in such a limited amount of time. Second, in an attempt to prepare students for later phases of their experience, we unwittingly ask students to possess a level of understanding that will not be developed until they are in the midst of the experience abroad. And where will we be when students are ready to have these discussions? While most of us attempt to provide opportunities for students to revisit their experience on return to campus, we sense that they need a more extensive follow-up that will allow them to truly process, integrate, and build on their study abroad experience. Unfortunately, we are rarely provided with the necessary resources to do just that. Finally, because of burgeoning participation in our study abroad programs, it is increasingly difficult to personalize the orientation process and to facilitate meaningful discussions that encourage critical thinking and responsibility on the part of the student.

This is why we have written *Study Abroad: How to Get the Most Out of Your Experience*. The three unique features of this book speak directly to the problems identified previously. First, its workbook format is personalized by its very nature and invites students to take an active role in their own preparation for the study abroad experience. It allows them to digest information at a pace with which they are comfortable and demands from them a critical exploration of their beliefs, goals, and behaviors. Moreover, it requires students to take responsibility for their personal, academic, and professional growth.

Second, this book joins students at each of the three crucial moments in their study abroad experience—before leaving home, while on-site, and after returning home—instead of a more traditional front-ended format that would force students to look at all phases of the experience at one time. That is, students complete exercises that are tailored to help them get the most out of the phase they are currently living.

Third, integration of this text into your existing orientation program requires little effort on your part. While this book would be ideal for a study abroad class, it can also be handed out to students to complete independently. We hope you will join us in the quest to help students move beyond the cliché of "expanding their horizons" and into a reality of globalizing their education.

PREFACE TO THE STUDENT

Having had the pleasure of studying abroad ourselves, we can honestly say that you are about to embark on a journey that has the potential to change your life. What we have found over the years is that study abroad is sometimes presented to students as an exotic experience and one that by design will surely lead to the fulfillment of "expanding their horizons." The idea tends to be that you will become more open-minded, independent, and adaptable. But we think it is important for you to know that mere participation in a study abroad program is very often not enough to ensure such outcomes.

Have you ever visited a new place but never left the proximity of your hotel? Or, if you left the hotel to attend a concert or visit a museum, did these experiences allow you the opportunity to learn how people there live? Unfortunately, it is very easy *not* to have a cross-cultural experience even though you are in a foreign country. It takes a purposeful agenda to move from being the conventional tourist to an explorer who truly acquires an authentic view of another culture.

This is why we have written *Study Abroad: How to Get the Most Out of Your Experience*. As you complete this workbook, we will accompany you on your journey, asking you key questions during crucial phases of your cross-cultural development. There are no right answers—only encouragement for a critical examination of what you want to get out of this experience, what challenges and accomplishments you encounter abroad, what personal growth is taking place, and what you are doing to make all of this happen. This workbook puts you in the driver's seat of your experience and encourages you to follow the roads less traveled.

GENERAL INFORMATION ABOUT THE TEXT

HOW THIS BOOK CAME TO BE

A few years ago, we (a study abroad coordinator and a faculty director from a foreign language department) got together to share ideas about how to improve the study abroad orientation for students going to Spain. Working closely with students studying abroad and having studied abroad ourselves, we saw great opportunity for improvement. We discovered that both of us were committed to facilitating a more effective cross-cultural experience and creating an instructional medium that other people like us could use for this purpose.

The original format was a class we designed and taught. We offered a trio of one-credit-hour courses taken at each phase of the study abroad experience: predeparture, on-site, and re-entry. As a pilot program, it was an optional experience that was in addition to our regular series of orientations for the study abroad experience. To our delight, most students chose to participate, and many of those who had gone through the program before we created the courses later expressed regret that they had not had the opportunity to participate (this after students in the courses told their friends about the kinds of activities and exercises involved).

While we were in the process of creating and piloting the courses, we held two truths simultaneously: first, that we believed that all study abroad students, regardless of program type, could benefit from this type of tailored experience and have a richer study abroad experience as a result and, second, that such special courses would be a possibility at some colleges and universities but would be seen as fiscally or otherwise impossible to implement at others. Presenting this course at NAFSA conferences, we confirmed both assumptions. Our colleagues agreed that such instruction would enhance the study abroad experience for students but also agreed that many institutions simply do not have the staff or the time to make this kind of commitment. On the basis of these realities, we changed our format, and this workbook is the result.

By integrating the basic ideas of our course into a self-directed workbook format, we saw that we could serve more students and provide a medium of instruction to a wider audience. This workbook can be integrated into study abroad programs that have a formal orientation course, or it can be used as a supplement to existing orientation programs or workshops. Furthermore, because of its workbook style, it can be used on an individual basis by students whose schools cannot offer much direction for this experience or by students who are simply committed to having a richer cross-cultural experience than their peers who do not use this text.

WORKBOOK DESIGN AND USE

The layout of our text was deliberate. We chose a workbook format because we hope that students will consider our ideas and add to them their own, thus creating for themselves a very personalized and critically examined record of their experience. Moreover, the division of the book into predeparture, on-site, and re-entry is designed to mirror the three significant phases of the endeavor, none of which should be left out. There is a time line included in the textbook that guides users to examine their journey at targeted periods, and directions at the beginning of each unit are given as to how to complete the exercises. While we feel that all the exercises will be beneficial to students, they are free to select those they find most helpful. As they complete exercises within each phase of the experience, they will be asked to reflect back to previous work. This purposeful design allows them not only to capture the thinking and feelings of one time but also to critically reflect on that period as they continue to plot their development. Exercises range from open-ended questions to information-gathering activities to student-generated professional projects. Appendix I of this text, "Implementation Tips for the Study Abroad Administrator/Faculty Director," is dedicated to helping the study abroad administrator and/or faculty director incorporate this workbook into existing orientations or classes.

We identified five distinct strands of development. They come from the foundational principles of our course and include personal development, learning about your own culture, learning about another culture, professional development, and learning another language. The order of these strands reflects our desire to focus the student's energy on the internal part of the experience (personal development) before moving on to the external parts of the experience (learning about another culture/learning another language). Thus, the placement of foreign language learning at the end of each strand should not be taken as a suggestion that it is of least importance. Its placement at the end was also a practical consideration, as we recognize that learning another language is not always part of a study abroad program.

WORKBOOK CONTENT

Let us tell you a bit more about each of the five strands chosen so that you will see why we consider each to be worthy of thought and investment. We treat them in the order in which they appear throughout the book.

Personal Development

Units in this strand walk students through the process of developing goals for the study abroad experience and assist them with identifying action plans to achieve those goals.

We assume that students who are using this text have already decided to study abroad and may have already begun to formulate general goals for the experience. For example, many students report a desire to expand their cultural horizons, to become fluent in another language, and/or to become more independent. Again, we want to stress that mere participation in a study abroad program is very often not enough to ensure such outcomes. Students will need to be very purposeful about the establishment of their goals as well as the development of specific steps in attaining them in order to find maximal success.

The on-site unit helps students examine how they feel once they are foreigners and gives them opportunities to work through any sense of culture shock they may be experiencing. The re-entry unit attempts to aid students in the often difficult moment of readjustment to their own country, school, family, and so forth and encourages them to incorporate some of the new traditions they have learned into their life at home.

Learning About Your Own Culture

Units in this strand facilitate an awareness of the impact the student's own culture has had on his or her way of thinking, behaving, and viewing the world.

Many students who are preparing to study abroad have never been to another country. It is only when they step out of their comfort zone that they begin to see it through different eyes. We hope to help students become more aware of the lens through which they have viewed the world up until now and in turn to be conscious of it as they travel abroad and then return home. Students may well be asked a variety of questions about the country they come from while abroad. For example, "Have you ever really thought about the images of the U.S. that the rest of the world receives via the U.S. media, American tourists, and U.S. foreign policies?" Many images are positive, but others can be quite negative.

We hope to encourage students to have a greater appreciation for our country while at the same time becoming more mindful of its shortcomings. Furthermore, we hope to help students focus attention on the cultural influences they take with them whenever they travel.

Learning About Another Culture

Units in this strand encourage students to intentionally seek experiences and information about their host culture. These experiences will contribute to their cross-cultural knowledge in a way that will result in a more authentic cultural understanding.

As we stated previously, one misconception about study abroad is that it necessarily leads to a cross-cultural experience. On the contrary, it is possible to continue familiar traditions, eating rituals, and social behaviors even while others around us participate differently. An "American ghetto," if you will, can provide an insular experience in which little adaptation is required. Furthermore, not only can students *not* experience another culture, but they can walk away from the experience having learned very little about their international hosts. For example, it is wholly possible to hold certain stereotyped beliefs before going abroad, subconsciously seek out examples in their support, and return home even more confident that these stereotypes are truths. When this happens, the individual has missed out on a fuller, more accurate understanding of the target culture and fails to contribute to international understanding by sharing this skewed perception with friends, family, and acquaintances.

We encourage students in these units to get out of their comfort zones and into the realm of cross-cultural adaptation and assimilation.

Professional Development

Units in this strand facilitate the development of a student-generated project that ties this time abroad to a future career, resulting in a tangible product that can be shared with a potential employer.

People often point to study abroad as one type of collegiate experience that will be impressive to prospective employers. But the reality is that study abroad has become so popular that merely mentioning (or including on a job résumé) that one has studied in another country does not distinguish him or her as much as it once did. Therefore, it seems to us that it is becoming all the more important for students to prove to a prospective employer that they have made the most of their experience abroad by tying it to their perceived future career. What tangible product will they be able to show this person?

For example, a political science major could research the political parties of the host country and create a presentation outlining their histories and principal differences. A business major might do a cross-cultural marketing review demonstrating how products in a given host country are advertised.

For students who don't yet know what type of job they want or change their mind before graduating, we say, "Don't worry." Whether or not the work they do in the area of professional development ends up matching the job for which they ultimately apply, it is sure to speak to their initiative, and that will likely impress prospective employers.

Learning Another Language

Units in this strand help students establish specific language-learning goals. While students are abroad, we suggest ways in which to wed both in-class and out-of-class experiences to those goals.

It is common for students to assume that on completion of their program they will be fluent in the target language (if, indeed, they go to a country in which languages other than English are spoken). Without getting into a long discussion of one's definition of the word "fluent," suffice it to say that this might or might not be an attainable goal. But one thing is certain: Any linguistic improvement will come only as a result of a well-planned and consistent effort on the students' part. We think that the word "planned" is key. Furthermore, our re-entry installment of this strand challenges students to keep up the language-learning momentum they acquired while abroad so that this, like the areas discussed in the other four strands, becomes a life-long process rather than the end of a finite experience.

Because this book is written for any college or university student who has chosen to study abroad, we recognize that some of these strands may seem more relevant to some students than others, depending on program type and individual goals. In fact, we see this as a strength of the book—it allows users to pick and choose strands and/or specific exercises suggested in each depending on personal goals. Or students may choose to explore all five strands and experience each in the predeparture, on-site, and re-entry phases.

USING THIS BOOK: A SUGGESTED TIME LINE

Below is a suggested time line that outlines when students should begin activities within the different phases of the study abroad experience.

Predeparture units were designed for students to complete in the prescribed order no later than two to four weeks prior to departure. Ideally, they should begin these exercises a couple of months prior to leaving the country. (Note: if you're on the plane and are just now getting a chance to take a look—don't let the previous suggestion stop you! Get started now!)

The **on-site** section allows for a more flexible approach as students are experiencing many things at one time. First, students should preview all five units prior to departure. It is crucial that they understand before leaving how they should record their experiences and language development, and also what cross-cultural activities the workbook suggests they pursue once abroad. Waiting until they are in the throes of adjusting to their new home can delay students' progress. Second, units can be formally completed by students (i.e., answering the questions for each exercise) at their desired pace once abroad. They will need to discipline themselves to complete the on-site activities as prescribed below.

1. Journal writing (including cross-cultural observations, language development and recording personal notes) should begin immediately and continue for the duration of the program.
2. Suggested cross-cultural activities should begin within the first or second week of the program and continue throughout (perhaps one to two activities per week).
3. Personal interest projects can be spread throughout the experience as desired. As part of a predeparture exercise, students will be asked to create a time line for completing their project. Once abroad, they should simply revisit that time line within the first week or two of their arrival in order to stay on schedule.

The first few **re-entry** activities are designed to be completed about one week prior to going home in order to help students start thinking about the upcoming transition. The rest of the exercises, however, should be visited one to two weeks after being at home. Finally, there are suggested activities in this unit that have no specified time line for completion. These activities were designed as vehicles that students can use to integrate their cross-cultural wisdom, professional development, and personal growth into their lives after they return home.

Let the journey begin!

ACKNOWLEDGMENTS

The authors would like to recognize the following people who helped make this book possible.

First and foremost, we want to thank our students. Without their enthusiasm, adventurous spirits, and willingness to share themselves, our study abroad course and subsequently this book would not have been possible. We also want to thank several colleagues at Illinois State University who were especially supportive. Dr. Bill Semlak's encouragement and his office's accommodations were key catalysts in this process. Dr. Kimberly Nance provided invaluable guidance during our proposal process for this book. Furthermore, Dr. Jonathan Rosenthal's encouragement and knowledge of the university bureaucracy helped get the class approved so that students could earn credit. We would also like to thank the Prentice Hall Modern Languages team, particularly our editor, Bob Hemmer, for his professional guidance and wonderful sense of humor throughout the process.

On a personal level, we want to thank all those who encourage us to be our best: our families, friends, our personal mentor, and each other. Without those close to us, we cannot find our internal sources of inspiration and wisdom.

Special thanks to the following reviewers for their wonderful insight: Diane Henker, University of Delaware, Dale Knickerbocker, East Carolina University; Nuria Novella, Middle Tennessee State University; Arthur R. Neisberg, University of Cincinnati; and William W. Cressey, Council on International Educational Exchange.

Finally, we want to thank you, the reader, for taking on the challenge of this workbook. The courage that is required to explore yourself and others can have a powerful impact. We wish you well on your journey.

Michele-Marie Dowell
Kelly P. Mirsky

Personal Development

" There were people on the trip who I could just tell went on the trip to say, 'I went to Spain!'——'What did you do?'—'Sat inside and watched TV . . . 'You know, like . . . 'What did you get out of it??!!' "

—*Samantha*

This unit will help you explore the reasons why you decided to study abroad and what personal goals you may want to accomplish during this experience. Many students say they want to learn about another culture, acquire foreign language skills, or become more "international" in our globalized world. Are these answers that have personal meaning, or are they politically correct responses? Sometimes students are drawn to studying abroad simply to get away from the mundane, to earn specific credit, or to have fun or just because their best friend is participating. The point of this unit is to stretch your level of expectation from the generic to something personally meaningful and attainable.

Exercises in this unit will encourage you to explore and begin creating concrete goals for this experience. In Exercise 1, we ask you to look at your choice to study abroad and what reasons, hopes, and experiences you bring to this decision. Exercise 2 asks you to articulate clearly your personal goals for study abroad and what actions you will take to accomplish them.

EXERCISE 1: THE CHOICE TO STUDY ABROAD

First, let's look at the reasons surrounding your decision to study abroad.

What made you choose to study abroad?

_____

_____

_____

_____

_____

What people were influential in making that decision (e.g., a professor, adviser, parent, friend)?

_____

_____

_____

_____

_____

In what country did you choose to study? Why did you choose that one?

_____

_____

_____

_____

_____

Next, let's examine what you hope to gain from this experience. What experiences abroad are you seeking (e.g., living in a bigger city, being close to a relative, being in a country in which a particular language is spoken)?

_____

_____

_____

_____

_____

What do you hope to learn as a result of the experience? In other words, how do you want to be able to talk to your peers, your family, or a professor about your experience when you return? For example, do you want to be able to say that you experienced Catholic Mass in Rome, that you understand farming in France better, or that you learned an effective teaching method in rural India?

_____

_____

_____

_____

_____

How are you expecting to grow personally from this experience? For example, students sometimes say they want to become more independent or to be able to problem solve more effectively.

_____

_____

_____

_____

_____

What are some personal qualities or values you hope might change as a result of this experience? For example, some students hope to open their minds to new ideas and ways of doing things, to view a different religion or form of government with more compassion and understanding, or to become more flexible.

_____

_____

_____

_____

_____

Finally, what would a "successful" study abroad experience look like? What would an "unsuccessful" study abroad experience look like? For example, how will you know if you're doing "well" abroad or if your program is going as you expected? Some students might characterize a successful experience as merely surviving it; others might define it in terms of intercultural friendships, not being homesick, or the amount of fun they have. What will you use to measure your success?

_____

_____

_____

_____

_____

Let's look at the impact an experience abroad naturally has on a person. How do you anticipate feeling while you are abroad? Imagine being in a foreign place, getting to know new people, not speaking the language, being far away from family and friends, and so on. How do you think factors like these will make you feel?

_____

_____

_____

_____

_____

What obstacles do you think will be challenging for you living and studying in a foreign country? List at least five and put them in the order of the least to the most stressful.

_____

_____

_____

_____

_____

What things do you think you will really enjoy while you're living and studying in a foreign country? List at least five and put them in the order of the least to the most enjoyable.

_____

_____

_____

_____

_____

Finally, let's look at what experiences you bring to this decision and how they might serve you abroad.

Have you been abroad before? If so, how does your previous experience compare with where you are going now? For example, being a tourist in Mexico for spring break is very different than living in a Mexican community and studying for a period of time.

_____

_____

_____

_____

How do you manage stress while you're at home? For example, what do you do when you've tried to complete an assignment but your computer crashes, the library doesn't have a research article you need, or you are having a disagreement with a roommate?

_____

_____

_____

_____

How do you think you will manage stress abroad when things you didn't expect to occur happen? Imagine, for example, that you are not making friends successfully, not earning good grades, or not having as much fun as you had hoped.

_____

_____

_____

_____

What other useful experiences do you bring to study abroad? For example, if you worked at a camp for six weeks and you were the only one who was not from that area, maybe you have gained some insight into how it feels to be an outsider in a new environment.

_____

_____

_____

_____

As you continue to develop, modify, and affirm your expectations for your study abroad experience, don't be surprised if they keep changing. Documenting where you are at the moment, like you just did, will create a benchmark for comparison. As you continue to complete these exercises during different phases of your experience, you will create for yourself a record of personal growth and change.

Now let's see how you can make your hopes a reality! We would like for you to form goals from your expectations. As you know, goals can serve as a map for navigating your experience. Again, merely being abroad does not automatically mean you will benefit from it as you hope. The point is to balance letting things happen naturally with creating a purposeful agenda.

EXERCISE 2: ESTABLISHING PERSONAL GOALS FOR STUDY ABROAD

Refering back to Exercise 1, list what you want to learn.

_____

_____

_____

_____

_____

Now, what can you do to learn these things? Think of specific activities.

_____

_____

_____

_____

_____

_____

_____

List how you want to change personally.

_____

_____

_____

_____

_____

_____

Now, what activities can you _do_ to facilitate these changes?

_____

_____

_____

_____

_____

_____

What experiences do you want to have?

_____

_____

_____

_____

_____

_____

Now, what can you *do* to make these experiences happen?

_____

_____

_____

_____

_____

_____

How do you want to deal with the stress that you will experience abroad? What can you *do* to incorporate these stress management techniques into your experience?

_____

_____

_____

_____

_____

_____

The next thing you need to do is to indicate how often you will engage in the activities you've identified (e.g., every day, once a week, once, twice).

Now complete the following formula with your previous answers:

In order to _____ (learn, experience, feel, and so on)
I will _____ (activities) _____ (frequency).

For example:

in order to <u>learn about daily life in Mexico:</u>

I will <u>read the local newspaper</u> <u>at least three days a week.</u>
I will <u>attend a local church</u> <u>at least two times a month.</u>
I will <u>shop at the local market</u> <u>at least once a week.</u>
I will <u>talk with my host family about their daily routine</u> <u>at least once a day.</u>

in order to <u>cope with the stress of culture shock:</u>

I will <u>run</u> <u>at least three days a week.</u>
I will <u>meditate in my room</u> <u>every morning.</u>

in order to <u>travel a lot during my experience:</u>

I will <u>travel to a nearby city</u> <u>at least every other weekend.</u>
I will <u>backpack in five different European countries</u> <u>during my two-week spring break.</u>

Write your goals here:

_____

_____

_____

_____

_____

_____

_____

_____

_____

_____

_____

_____

NOTE

_____
You may want to record contact information for friends and family you want
to remain in touch with while you're studying abroad. Take a look at Appendix 3. There you will find an address book for your convenience.

Learning About Your Own Culture

"A lot of Europeans know more about America than a lot of Americans do, and that's what I think is really embarrassing."

—Samantha

"They'll be

whipping out facts left and right about their countries, about the government, the history—anything. And then they'll ask me [about the U.S.] and I'll be like, 'ehhh . . .' "

—Donna

This unit will help raise your awareness about rituals, traditions, and foundational principles of the U.S. We want you to consider some of these familiar things with the idea of being able to explain them to someone in your host culture. Students often report that people in their host country knew more about the U.S. than they did. They also noticed that people turned to them as "Americans" to explain issues about the U.S. that were on the television or in newspapers. In some instances, discussions were intense debates in classrooms or around the table at dinner. We want you to educate and in some cases reeducate yourself about your country so that you can be an informed ambassador while abroad.

Exercise 3 gives you scenarios that address some issues you may encounter abroad, specifically regarding information about the U.S. and your culture. We ask that you outline a response that addresses the issue at hand, keeping in mind that you are talking with someone who may or may not understand your background. Some scenarios will require that you draw on your own experience, making them fairly easy to answer; others may require some investigation. Each scenario is followed by related questions that we encourage you to consider and discuss with fellow travelers, professors, or friends and family. They are meant to serve as catalysts for further exploration. It is hoped that this exercise encourages you to seek out information about the U.S. and to pay closer attention to current domestic and international events.

EXERCISE 3: WHAT DOES IT MEAN TO BE AN AMERICAN?

Let's look at some issues relating to the U.S. that you might be asked about while abroad.

ALL AMERICAN?

You are waiting in a bus terminal, and you strike up a conversation with a fellow passenger. This person asks, "Where are you from?" You reply, "America." He says jokingly, "Which one?" You feel embarrassed and reply, "The U.S.; North America." You board the bus for the six-hour journey during which this same guy sits next to you. During the course of the trip you embark on a long discussion about origin. He is from Germany and has traveled to the U.S. several times to visit some family. At one point in the discussion, he asks, "If most Americans are born in America, why do some people make the distinction between American, African American, Asian American, and so on? My mother is from Austria, and I don't say I'm an Austrian German?" How would you respond to this question?

_____

_____

_____

_____

_____

_____

_____

_____

_____

_____

_____

_____

_____

_____

_____

QUESTIONS FOR FURTHER EXPLORATION:

How would you explain what it means to be American?

Where does your family come from?

How does your origin affect your sense of identity?

How would you explain the various "American" identities—a melting pot? a salad bowl?

GOVERNMENT

You have been invited to a family gathering for dinner. While eating, an uncle asks, "How do you feel about the current president of the U.S.?" He adds, "We were really hoping for the opposing candidate and wondered if some people in the U.S. were also disappointed. Were they?" How would you respond?

_____

_____

_____

_____

_____

_____

_____

_____

_____

_____

_____

_____

_____

QUESTIONS FOR FURTHER EXPLORATION:

How would you explain the major political parties?

How would you explain the electoral process?

What is the administrative structure of our government? How would you explain the House of Representatives, the Senate, Congress, and the president's cabinet?

RELIGION

You go with a friend to a place of worship that is new to you. You are asking a lot of questions to understand the religious beliefs of this group of people, and you ask the meaning behind the different rituals you have observed. On the way home from worship, your friend begins to ask you about your religious beliefs and the rituals that surround them. Your friend also has heard of rituals, such as the Easter Bunny and Passover, but is confused as to their meaning.

How would you explain your religious beliefs or any spiritual views you hold? Can you explain common symbols (e.g., crosses or stars), religious rituals (going to church or synagogue), holiday celebrations, and the history of your belief system?

_____

_____

_____

_____

_____

_____

_____

_____

_____

_____

_____

_____

_____

_____

_____

_____

_____

_____

_____

_____

_____

QUESTIONS FOR FURTHER EXPLORATION:

What religions are practiced in the U.S.?

What does separation of church and state mean?

SOCIAL ISSUES

You are in class, and the discussion is about health care. A classmate asks, "How can Americans justify charging people an exorbitant amount of money for insurance in order to receive medical treatment? The insurance companies make the decisions as opposed to the doctors. Why don't they adopt a socialized health care system like in this country?" How would you respond?

_____

_____

_____

_____

_____

_____

_____

_____

QUESTIONS FOR FURTHER EXPLORATION:

How would you explain the health care system in the U.S.?

What are the major issues surrounding abortion?

How is the gay and lesbian population treated?

What are the major issues surrounding class?

What are the major issues surrounding racial and ethnic groups?

What services are provided to the mentally ill?

HISTORY

Your host mom is a big fan of American history. She is particularly fascinated with Thomas Jefferson because he was one of the authors of the Declaration of Independence. She asks, "Have you ever visited his home in Monticello, Virginia?" She also jokes with you and says, "Your American history class was probably the shortest course you ever took."

How would you accept this invitation to discuss your country's history? Do you know how our country was founded? Do you know principles behind the Declaration of Independence?

_____

_____

_____

_____

_____

_____

_____

_____

_____

_____

_____

_____

QUESTIONS FOR FURTHER EXPLORATION:

How old is our country?

What major wars have taken place in the U.S. and with whom? What were they fighting about?

Can you name at least three major political or social leaders who had significant influence on this country?

ECONOMY

A child you are tutoring in school asks, "Do you have a mansion for a house? I was watching the television, and I saw that everyone had gigantic houses like the movie stars in California! Are you one of the rich Americans my grandpa always talks about?" What responses could you provide him?

_____

_____

_____

_____

_____

_____

_____

_____

_____

QUESTIONS FOR FURTHER EXPLORATION:

What are some signs of poverty in the U.S.?

What programs does the U.S. provide to support low-income families?

Do rich people keep getting richer and poor people keep getting poorer?

What currency do we use? How does that compare with the currency of your host culture?

INTERNATIONAL RELATIONS

A group of friends from class go out for a cup of coffee. The discussion turns to the Middle East and how the U.S. provided such a disservice to the Afghan people when they were fighting the Soviets. They accuse the U.S. of once again putting its nose into other people's business. How would you contribute to this conversation? What is your opinion of the U.S.'s role in the world?

_____

_____

_____

_____

_____

_____

_____

_____

_____

_____

_____

_____

QUESTIONS FOR FURTHER EXPLORATION:

Who are our allies?

Who are our enemies? Why?

What role is the U.S. playing in current international events?

RESOURCES

Your host mom keeps turning lights off behind you. She literally suggests that when you go from your bedroom to the bathroom, you turn off your light. You ask her, "Is electricity here very expensive?" She responds, "It's extremely costly." She later comments, "I imagine it must be so different for you living here because at home you have your own car, you can leave the lights on and have plenty of hot water, and no one is worrying about whether or not there will be the same resources tomorrow." How would you respond to this comment?

QUESTIONS FOR FURTHER EXPLORATION:

Do you think that the average U.S. citizen makes efforts to conserve energy? How? Does he or she try to preserve the environment? How?

SPORTS AND LEISURE

A classmate asks if you ever spend time with your family. She says that her dad said that all people do in the U.S. is work and watch American football. How would you respond to this?

_____

_____

_____

_____

_____

_____

QUESTIONS FOR FURTHER EXPLORATION:

How do people here spend their time when they are not working?

What are some popular sports?

Can you explain the rituals associated with American football?

MEDIA

Your host dad said he was in the U.S. for business one time and thought the news was strictly for entertainment. He said anchors seemed to joke with fellow newscasters like they were good friends. He also wondered why he had a hard time finding international news coverage—all he heard about was the U.S. and local current events. How would you respond to his experience?

_____

_____

_____

_____

_____

_____

_____

_____

_____

_____

QUESTIONS FOR FURTHER EXPLORATION:

What are the major television networks?

What themes are covered in a typical news broadcast?

To what extent is international news covered?

CRIME AND SECURITY

During orientation, your study abroad adviser reviewed safety issues to consider while abroad. She said that you are more likely to get pickpocketed abroad than to be seriously injured or killed. Your host mom also reminds you to keep your wallet hidden so as to not draw attention to potential thieves. She asks, "Don't you have to worry about these things at home?" How would you respond to this question?

_____

_____

_____

_____

_____

_____

_____

_____

_____

_____

_____

_____

QUESTIONS FOR FURTHER EXPLORATION:

What measures do you take to keep yourself safe at home?

How would you explain the process of being arrested, charged with a crime, and then punished?

Why are guns not against the law?

What security measures do cities and towns make to keep people safe?

What national security measures does the U.S. take?

EDUCATION

A professor makes a comment in class that feels insulting to you. He suggests that higher education in the U.S. is far less prestigious than elsewhere in the world because anybody can get a college education. He says that he doesn't understand why this experience isn't reserved for the most intelligent and capable of students and why we would water down our curriculum to let everyone in. How do you feel about his observation? How would you respond?

_____

_____

_____

_____

_____

_____

_____

_____

_____

_____

_____

_____

_____

_____

_____

_____

_____

_____

QUESTIONS FOR FURTHER EXPLORATION:

How are students evaluated in the classroom?

What kind of relationship exists between the student and teacher (e.g., formal or informal)?

What are the issues surrounding education in the U.S.?

PERSONAL

What makes you proud of the U.S.?

What issues embarrass you about our country?

Learning About Another Culture

"I have observed that calendars are different. The first day of the week is Monday, not Sunday—like in the U.S."

—*Andrea*

"*In general,* I believe that young people [abroad] know a lot more about the world of politics than young people in the United States do."

—Jeff

In this unit, we will help you start thinking about the ways in which you will be learning about your host culture. While many students think that this process begins when they get off the plane, we believe it should begin well before then. In Exercise 4, we suggest one way that you might prepare yourself by doing some fact-finding about your host country. We think that you will find your time abroad better spent with a relatively strong background on which to build. In Exercise 5, we ask you to pause to consider the difference between fact and opinion as you begin your quest to "know" your host culture. Exercise 6 is an introduction to journal writing. This is just an introduction, as more will be said about journaling in Units 5, 10, and 15 on language learning.

EXERCISE 4: RESEARCHING POLITICAL, HISTORICAL, AND CULTURAL INFORMATION ABOUT YOUR HOST SITE

In this activity, we ask you to learn a bit about each of a wide variety of topics relating to your host culture. We used to use this activity with our students who were preparing to study in Madrid, Spain. They were often surprised at how little they really knew about some of the topics, even though many were already Spanish majors and minors. Learning more now (or proving to yourself that you already know quite a bit) should help you feel more grounded once you arrive in your host culture. Citizens of other countries often know a great deal more about the U.S. than we do about their countries, such that your knowledge of the host culture will likely be seen as a sign of respect by many.

In completing this exercise, use any source of information to which you have access, such as newspapers, magazines, television, and the Internet. Don't worry if you can't answer some questions at all or have very limited answers to others. We will revisit this information once you are abroad, and you will have another opportunity to fill in any blanks.

I. Government

1. What type of government does this country have?

2. Who is currently the country's leader?

3. Do you know what he or she looks like?

4. Name the major political parties and describe their basic platforms.

5. Which party is in power at the present?

6. Which party was last in power?

7. Describe several current events that are important to this country.

II. Economy

1. What is the name of the currency in this country?

2. In what denominations do bills exist? Coins?

3. What is the current exchange rate?

III. Education

1. How is the K–12 educational system structured? At what age do children begin school?

_____

_____

2. Are there both public and private schools? Which is more common?

_____

3. What is the structure of the college/university system?

_____

_____

4. What are the requirements to enter?

_____

_____

5. How much does it cost to attend?

_____

6. What kinds of courses are available? Do students have majors and minors like we do?

_____

_____

7. How is the grading system structured (e.g., A,B,C,D,F)?

_____

_____

8. How long does it take to graduate? What is the degree called? (Is there only one possible undergraduate degree?)

_____

_____

9. Do students tend to study in their hometowns or travel elsewhere?

_____

_____

IV. History and Geography

1. Give a *brief* summary of the history of this country, focusing on the events that most clearly impact present-day life.

_____

_____

_____

_____

_____

2. In Appendix 7, you are encouraged to find a map of the country and make a copy small enough to glue or tape into the book for future reference. Now describe how the country is organized politically (i.e., divided into states, provinces, and so on).

_____

_____

_____

3. Name the largest cities in the country and briefly describe each.

_____

_____

_____

_____

_____

_____

4. If it is not among the cities you described in item 3, what do you know about the city in which you will be living?

_____

_____

_____

_____

V. Food and Meal Schedules

1. At what time are daily meals served in this country?

   _____

2. Of what does each meal typically consist?

   _____

   _____

3. Name several common main dishes served.

   _____

   _____

4. Name several desserts common to this country.

   _____

   _____

5. Name famous regional dishes and identify the regions of the country from which they come.

   _____

   _____

   _____

   _____

6. How expensive is food in grocery stores? Is it more or less expensive than in the U.S.? What types of food are available?

   _____

   _____

   _____

   _____

VI. Daily Life

1. What forms of transportation are available in the city in which you will be living? Are they expensive to use? Which are most common?

   _____

   _____

2. What is the pace of daily life? On what do you base your answer?

   _____

   _____

   _____

VII. Culture
Religion

1. What are the main religions practiced in this country?

_____

_____

_____

_____

2. In what ways does one see their influence in daily life?

_____

_____

_____

_____

_____

Holidays

1. What are the main holidays in this country? When do they take place? What is their history? Where do they take place (i.e., all over the country, or in just one location)? In order to organize your answer, we have provided a list of the months of the year.

January

_____

February

_____

March

_____

April

_____

May

_____

_____

June

July

August

September

October

November

December

Music

1. What is the traditional music of this country?

2. Do they have music that is similar to what you listen to in the U.S.?

3. Name several current singers and/or musical groups (who are native to the country).

4. Are some of the bands you listen to here in the U.S. also popular there?

_____

Art/Architecture

1. Name at least three famous artists and describe the kind of work they do/did.

   1. _____

   2. _____

   3. _____

2. What kind of architecture exists in this country? Does it vary by region? If so, how?

   _____

   _____

   _____

3. What role does history play in this country's architecture?

   _____

   _____

Literature/Film/Press

1. Name at least three famous writers and identify their genre and a famous work of theirs.

   1. _____

   2. _____

   3. _____

2. Name at least one famous film director and several of his or her works.

   _____

3. Name at least one famous actor (excluding those currently acting in the U.S.).

   _____

4. Do films in this country follow the same general formulas as those in the U.S.? If not, how do they differ?

   _____

5. Name the newspapers of widest readership in this country.

   _____

   _____

   _____

Sports

1. What sports are played in this country? Are they similar to those in the U.S.?

_____

_____

_____

2. List and describe the three most popular sports.

1. _____

2. _____

3. _____

3. What role do sports appear to play in this country's culture?

_____

_____

Self-Awareness

1. About what aspects of their country are host nationals proud?

_____

_____

_____

_____

2. About what issues are they concerned?

_____

_____

_____

_____

VIII. Health and Safety

1. If a possession such as your wallet or purse is lost or stolen while you are studying abroad, whom will you contact?

_____

_____

2. If the item that is lost or stolen is your passport, how could you replace it?

_____

_____

3. If you have a medical emergency, whom will you contact?

_____

_____

4. Does the U.S. State Department make any recommendations about safety and health precautions for those traveling to your host country?

_____

_____

_____

5. What about the Centers for Disease Control? Do they suggest any immunizations or other health precautions?

_____

_____

_____

For your future reference, you may want to list the sources you used to obtain your information. You may wish to revisit them on your return or share them with future sojourners traveling to your host country.

EXERCISE 5: UNDERSTANDING THE DIFFERENCE BETWEEN FACT AND OPINION IN THE CONTEXT OF OTHER CULTURES

In today's world, opinions are often expressed as if they were facts, and it can be difficult to distinguish between the two. The ability to make that distinction is important in that if we can at least identify an idea as an opinion, we can make the conscious choice to believe it or not as we see fit. If, on the other hand, we treat all incoming information relating to our host country as factual, we cheat ourselves of the opportunity to form our own impressions. For this exercise, you will need a book, a magazine article, or any other source dealing with your host country. Flip to any page of the source material and read an entire paragraph without stopping. Now go back and read the same paragraph one sentence at a time. Looking at each given sentence, ask yourself if the information is factual (could be corroborated by many other sources) or the opinion of the author. Once you finish the process for the whole paragraph, reflect on the reading. Was all information factual, all opinion, or a combination thereof? Did you get the same impression of the information from both readings, or did you come away with a different sense the second time? No matter how the exercise turned out for you, we hope that it encourages you to be a critical reviewer of information that you receive about your host culture and make a clear distinction between facts and your own opinions when it comes time to share information about this host culture with others.

EXERCISE 6: INTRODUCTION TO ON-SITE JOURNALING

Do you already keep a journal? Many of us do, while others either find it too time consuming or simply are not interested. Whichever is the case, you will want to keep a journal while abroad, as this experience will be one you will want to savor in years to come. There are many ways to go about keeping a journal, and you will certainly want to choose the style that works best for you. What kinds of information seem appropriate to include in your study abroad journal?

_____

_____

_____

How often should you write in it?

_____

We would like to suggest that you consider making an effort to write at least a brief entry each day and that you include a minimum of one cross-cultural observation in each journal entry. You will be glad that you put the effort into your journal. Former students typically report considering their journals as among the most treasured artifacts of their trip!

NOTE

Now would be a good time to look ahead at Appendix 8. You will see how we have structured the journal pages.

Unit 4

Professional Development

"This project has made me more interested in going to Spain because now I am able to combine two areas of interest together—Spanish and art."

—*Lisa*

In this unit, we will explore ways in which your study abroad experience may enhance your future career. Whether you intend to join the workforce on graduation or pursue graduate studies, these activities will help you identify and take advantage of the professional opportunities inherent in a study abroad experience.

EXERCISE 7: ESTABLISHING PROFESSIONAL GOALS FOR STUDY ABROAD

You will first want to identify your professional goals. When you do so, be as specific as possible. For example, instead of saying, "My professional goal is to get a job in international business," you might say, "My professional goal is to get a job in an import-export business." List your career goals as you now envision them. If you are still thinking about several different careers, list the goals that would be associated with each.

_____

_____

_____

_____

_____

Just as you did earlier for your personal goals, brainstorm specific ways in which you might work toward each professional goal while abroad.

_____

_____

_____

_____

_____

_____

EXERCISE 8: THE RÉSUMÉ AND JOB INTERVIEW

Of course, you will not know until you are in your host country whether all your professionally related ideas can be carried out. Do not worry about that for now. Now imagine that you are preparing for the job market. First, you want to figure out how best to characterize your experience abroad on your résumé. What would you like to be able to say? *For example, our student, Andrea, might say something like, "I studied the ways in which print and television advertising differ between Spain and the U.S., with particular focus on images of the body in advertising."*

_____

_____

_____

_____

_____

How can you make the statement you just wrote a reality?

_____

_____

_____

_____

Next, think about the types of questions that an interviewer is likely to ask, such as what kinds of professional experiences you have had that relate to the position in question. What would you like to be able to say about your study abroad experience in answer to such questions?

_____

_____

_____

_____

_____

In the following exercise, we want you to consider one way of going about learning more about your professional field while abroad.

EXERCISE 9: THE PROFESSIONAL INTEREST PROJECT

This project is designed to help you capitalize on your experience professionally and may span the duration of your time abroad. Most people do not think about doing such projects unless they are class assignments. But we think that they are an excellent way to focus your energies abroad constructively while still leaving ample time for fun. The beauty of this exercise is that you can make it as elaborate or as simple as you wish since it is just for you. Remember to take into account your answers to the previous exercises when planning the project.

We begin by giving two project examples based on the experiences of our own students in Spain. You will notice that they contrast markedly. Jeff's professional interest project did not relate to his major in school. He had several interests, and this project explored his entrepreneurial side. Lisa, on the other hand, chose to link her project to her major in school.

EXAMPLE 1: JEFF

Jeff was a college sophomore majoring in math education. He was about to spend a semester in Madrid and wanted to tie in his experiences there with his future goal of becoming an entrepreneur who does business internationally. So he decided to research aspects of the business world in Spain.

EXAMPLE 2: LISA

Lisa was a college junior majoring in art education. She, too, was preparing to spend a semester in Madrid. Lisa hoped to become an art teacher on graduation, so she decided to learn as much as possible about folk art in Spain to use in her future lessons.

Now it's your turn. Take a few moments to list some ideas for your project. Remember that these are just to get you started.

_____

_____

_____

_____

_____

Once you have decided on a project idea, try filling in the following information for the topic you are thinking about pursuing. You might recognize the format as typical of what proposal writers in any field might use. Sticking to the format will help you become more refined in your plan and make it easier to tell how realistic the plan is.

1. **Project Statement** In this section, you want to briefly state what you intend to do. What is the reason for completing the project? For example, a synopsis of Jeff's project statement follows:

The purpose of this project is to explore business dealings in Spain. . . . As the Internet and international business opportunities become more widely available, the ability to learn all one can about an associate's culture and society before any business contact begins becomes crucial for future success. Lisa, on the other hand, stated, *I will be concentrating on the folk art of Spanish potters. I will be researching the techniques and methods that they use in the building of certain functional pottery. I will also be finding out what kinds of styles are used in different areas of Spain.*

Try formulating your own project statement here.

_____

_____

_____

_____

_____

2. **Objectives** Jeff decided that his specific objectives were the following:

1. *To learn how Spanish businesspeople negotiate friendship and business relations among themselves*
2. *To learn the norms associated with Spanish business practices*
3. *To establish business contacts for future dealings in Spain*

Lisa's objectives consisted of the following:

1. *To determine the basic techniques and methods used in Spanish pottery making*
2. *To determine the designs and color schemes used in the pottery of different regions of Spain*
3. *To create a sample piece of Spanish-style pottery while in Spain*
4. *To create a lesson plan to be used in future art classes*

Now list your specific objectives in doing the project. What exactly do you plan to accomplish?

1. _____

2. _____

3. _____

4. _____

5. _____

6. _____

7. _____

8. _____

3. **Specific Actions**   These are the specific steps you will take in carrying out the project. It may well be the most important element of your proposal because it is your opportunity to see whether the project can really be accomplished. _For example, Jeff's plan consisted of first contacting five to ten business people and asking if they would be willing to participate in a videotaped interview. One of Lisa's first steps was to spend time at a museum in Madrid studying and sketching pieces of pottery._

List all the steps you plan to take as if you need to convince someone else how well thought-out the project really is. Include targeted dates for completion for each task. This will give you a clear time line for the project.

1. _____

2. _____

3. _____

4. _____

5. _____

6. _____

7. _____

8. _____

9. _____

10. _____

4. **Outcomes**   What will you actually produce as a result of your project? Or does having a tangible product even matter to you? This will depend to a great extent on your topic and goals for doing the project. But remember that if it is for professional purposes, a tangible product is advisable. _Jeff planned to produce a video capturing five to ten interviews with Spanish businesspeople and chronicling a typical day in the life of a Spanish businessperson. In addition, he hoped to create a detailed handbook containing other pertinent information and a list of people he met in Spain who wanted to start a business relationship with someone in the U.S. Lisa planned to create a book of sketches of the styles of pottery found throughout Spain, write a lesson plan appropriate for her future students, and make a sample piece of Spanish-style pottery._

What will your outcomes be?

1. _____

2. _____

3. _____

4. _____

5. _____

6. _____

5. **Audience**   Who might be interested in hearing about or seeing your project once it is finished? Maybe it will be something private that you do just for your own enjoyment or learning. But if not, someone with similar interests is bound to want to know what you learned. List any possible audiences, including employers or future classes, if you plan to teach. *Jeff thought that the list of Spanish business contacts could be useful to his business associates in the U.S. Lisa not only planned to use her lesson plan in the future when she gets a teaching job but also thought she might incorporate it into a lesson she teaches to local children through one of her university art classes.*

Who might your audience be?

_____

_____

_____

_____

_____

6. **Equipment and Expenses**   Will this project cost any money to complete? List any possible related expenses here. Think about such items as transportation, photocopying, cameras, video- or audiotaping equipment, film, or other expenses. *For Jeff, expenses included a camcorder, blank videotapes, and batteries, whereas Lisa needed to purchase a sketchbook and be prepared to pay any fees associated with the use of a pottery studio while in Spain (such as clay, studio time, and firing of the pottery).*

What will your costs be?

1. _____

2. _____

3. _____

4. _____

5. _____

6. _____

Now look back over your answers. If you like what you see, you're on your way. If not, either refine the topic or choose another one. What is most important is to pick something that is both meaningful to you and researchable in your host country.

Learning Another Language

"I got off the plane, and I'm going up the escalator to get my bags, and these Spanish girls——university students——started asking me questions, and I'd try to spit out a response, and I couldn't. And I'm like, 'Why did I think I could go through a whole semester, almost a year, without any Spanish?' "

—Jeff

If your study abroad program entails learning the language of the host country, the three units in this strand should be of interest to you. But if there is no official language-learning component to your program, you will want to decide whether you wish to pursue this goal on your own. If you do, you will be able to complete the recommended exercises, perhaps modifying them in ways that make sense to you.

In this unit, you will first focus on establishing your language learning-goals in Exercise 10. Exercise 11 is designed to help you identify situations that might serve to hinder your efforts to accomplish your goals and to challenge you to brainstorm possible solutions. Exercise 12 rounds out the unit and is designed to encourage you to begin your language-learning odyssey now—before you have even left home.

EXERCISE 10: ESTABLISHING LANGUAGE-LEARNING GOALS FOR STUDY ABROAD

If you are going to be in a formal language-learning context, there will certainly be goals established for you in your language courses. But in this exercise, we ask that you begin to consider your personal language-learning goals for both in and out of class. We realize that students going abroad represent a wide range of proficiency levels in the foreign language, so we have structured this strand in such a way as to speak to each student at their current level of expertise and challenge them to reach greater heights.

As stated in the goal-setting exercises in earlier units, it is important to be as specific as possible in the wording of your goals and equally important to identify the particular steps or tasks that you plan to use in order to reach your goals.

So, first we ask that you list your language-learning goals. In identifying them, you may choose to consider the following broad categories:

Listening comprehension
Reading comprehension
Ability to speak the language
Ability to write in the language

Or you may choose to focus on specific aspects such as the following:

- Knowledge of the formal grammar of the language
- Ability to understand slang or more colloquial speech
- Vocabulary development
- Pronunciation

- Fluidity of speech
- Ability to understand and identify regional dialects

	Goal	Specific Steps in Reaching Goal
1.		
2.		
3.		
4.		
5.		
6.		
7.		
8.		

Now that you have listed your goals, go back and write in as many possible steps as you can think of that might help you reach each goal while abroad. *For example, to attain her goal to "increase fluency in Spanish," our student, Samantha, proposed the following two steps: first, to "pick up on little details of the language" and, second, to "speak Spanish when talking with English-speaking people."*

Remember that this is just a first attempt at goal setting—you can review your goals and action steps at any time and modify them as you see fit.

EXERCISE 11: IDENTIFYING POSSIBLE ROADBLOCKS TO ACHIEVING LANGUAGE-LEARNING GOALS

Another topic to which you will want to give some thought before leaving is how/when you plan to use the target language once abroad. While it is extremely common for students to announce beforehand that they will speak nothing but the foreign language while abroad, in reality many do not follow through for a variety of reasons. *For example, on her return from Spain, Samantha said the following about her language-learning goal of increased fluency: "I didn't speak Spanish with English-speaking people, but I did increase my fluency greatly."*

Depending on the program format, your personality, and a host of other factors, it may not be realistic to place this lofty expectation on yourself. If you want to get the very most linguistically out of your time abroad, you will certainly want to consider this option. But you may have to give up certain things in order to attain it. For example, classmates and others may not want to spend as much time with you as you would like if they have no opportunities to fall back on the comfort and ease of their native language when they are around you. Whatever you decide, just be sure that your goals for personal development (as established in Exercise 2) and your language-learning goals do not conflict.

Think about the following:

1. How are you going to manage your own personal language-learning goals within groups that may choose not to speak the target language?

_____

_____

_____

_____

_____

_____

_____

2. We have identified one common situation that can cause difficulties for students who wish to fully immerse themselves in the target language while abroad. What other possible challenges do you foresee while accomplishing your language-learning goals?

_____

_____

_____

_____

_____

_____

3. Can you envision solutions for these challenges?

_____

_____

_____

EXERCISE 12: JUMP-STARTING YOUR LANGUAGE-LEARNING EXPERIENCE

Once you have finished identifying your goals and how you plan to address them once you get to your host country, it is time to ask yourself one more question:

What can I do now to begin to address these goals?

You may find that you can actually get started now. For example, if one of your goals is to feel more confident in using the language when conversing with native speakers, you could begin a vocabulary list of the kinds of things you would likely need to express, maybe organized thematically. If you will be staying with a host family, list the types of foods you love as well as those you do not care for. Most important, list any to which you are allergic! You will certainly want to be able to convey this information to a host family as well as others who will be in charge of your meals (even in restaurants). While many students learn basic food vocabulary in class, many do not have a wide vocabulary in this area. Now is the time to prepare!

List three to five ways you can begin (or have already begun) preparing now:

1. _____
2. _____
3. _____
4. _____
5. _____

NOTE

Look ahead at Appendix 8 to see how we ask you to record your language-learning experience while abroad.

Before you leave,

be sure to check out the appendices. There you will be asked to address practical issues such as packing, money matters, extracurricular travel, and other personal matters that will need attending to while you are gone.

We also suggest that you preview the five on-site units now because you will be working on them simultaneously rather than in chronological order. All should be started right away once you arrive.

Now that you are
abroad . . .

Personal Development

"I just figured it had to be culture shock I was feeling. . . . It felt a little overwhelming . . . all of a sudden I just felt alone in this country."

—*Lisa*

"After two

or three weeks, that's when it hit me....
I came to a point where I wanted to go
home; I didn't want to be there any more.
But then I got over that and was fine."

—Beth

In this unit, we want to explore how you are feeling about your host culture and how you are managing your culture shock. It is common for students to have overestimated how "great" it is to be a foreigner in a different country. Many students report experiencing isolation, sadness, and frustration as they grapple with maintaining their identity and adapting to a new environment. Without careful examination, discomfort (no matter how subtle) can cause you to make choices that keep you on your familiar ground. For example, if you're doing everything you usually do at home except that the local bar is now a pub in London, you may not be stretching outside of your comfort zone. This is exactly what we mean when we say that it is easy *not* to have a cross-cultural experience even though you are in a foreign country. Personal growth often requires treading in unfamiliar territory and attempting to be successful in the way success is defined locally. If the locals are taking public transportation that stops several blocks before their place of employment, we encourage you not to bypass this ritual by taking a taxi door to door. The point of study abroad is to try on local traditions, values, and behaviors of the host culture (provided that you feel safe doing so) until they almost feel like "home." It takes a purposeful agenda to move from being the conventional tourist to an explorer who truly acquires an authentic view of another culture.

Therefore, we offer exercises that help you be more of an "explorer." Exercise 13 asks you to examine your perceptions of your host culture, ways in which you are interacting with the locals, and how people are treating you. Exercise 14 asks you to explore how you're feeling about your new environment and being away from home. Finally, Exercise 15 asks you to report how you are changing your behavior to adapt to your current situation.

EXERCISE 13: BEING A FOREIGNER

Remember in Exercise 1 when we asked you to think about what you *thought* you would like about your host culture and what you *thought* you wouldn't? Let's revisit those areas now that you're actually there.

What *do* you like about your new environment?

_____

_____

_____

What *don't* you like about your new environment?

_____

_____

_____

How do the likes and dislikes you listed compare to your predictions in Exercise 1?

_____

_____

_____

What other things do you want to make note of about your new environment?

_____

_____

_____

Let's transition to exploring your social "position" in this new place. You are a student on a study abroad program—not quite a tourist but not a local, either. What does this mean in practical terms?

Do the locals know you're a foreigner? How? What do you say, do, or look like that gives them that impression?

_____

_____

_____

_____

_____

How do the locals respond to you? For example, some students who have been abroad report that they feel like they stand out or that people stare at them because they look different. What has your experience been like? Explain how locals speak to you. Explain how they look at you.

_____

_____

_____

_____

_____

How much contact are you having with the locals? For example, what opportunities do you have during the day to interact with people from this area (e.g., in public places, your host family's house, or in class)?

_____

_____

_____

_____

Does this contact allow you to learn about the local culture?

_____

_____

_____

_____

If you were to make a checklist for comparing the local culture with your culture, how would it look in terms of the following categories?

Use of time (leisure time versus working; punctuality):

_____

_____

_____

_____

Use of space (personal or public):

_____

_____

_____

_____

What people generally wear every day (for work, school, or special occasions):

_____

_____

_____

_____

What religious beliefs are held (if any) and what rituals are practiced:

_____

_____

_____

_____

What people do for fun:

_____

_____

_____

_____

How people spend their money:

_____

_____

_____

_____

What constitutes a family:

_____

_____

_____

_____

How people engage in politics and if they are discussed:

_____

_____

_____

_____

Other areas you feel a sense of similarity or difference:

_____

_____

_____

_____

What has being a foreigner taught you about yourself or others?

_____

_____

_____

_____

_____

If you had to describe what it feels like to be a foreigner to someone who has never traveled, how would you describe it?

_____

_____

_____

_____

There are many different ways people react to being in a new environment. Emotions can range from pure excitement to fear to confusion to frustration. "Culture shock" is the term generally used to describe this spectrum of reactions. It's also important to note that success as a sojourner abroad is not necessarily defined by whether you feel bothered by doing things differently. There is no "right" way to react. So, how are you?

EXERCISE 14: WORKING THROUGH CULTURE SHOCK

Let's look at how you have had to change your behavior and then how you are responding to this new set of circumstances. First, think in terms of your daily routine and other common activities. For each of the following categories explain how the activity differs while you're abroad from when you are at home.

Waking up:

_____

_____

Getting ready (e.g., using the toilet, bathing, using the water, and so on):

_____

_____

Eating breakfast:

_____

_____

Getting to school:

_____

_____

The classroom (e.g., relationship with your professors, homework, class participation, lectures, grading, and so on):

_____

_____

_____

_____

Where you do your homework (e.g., resources, computers, and so on):

_____

_____

_____

_____

Options for leisure time:

_____

_____

_____

Interactions with friends:

Interactions with family:

Eating dinner:

Going to bed/sleeping:

Banking:

Shopping:

Going to a restaurant:

Using public transportation/driving:

Using the telephone:

Using the Internet:

Working/earning money:

Traveling:

Drinking alcohol, smoking, caffeine intake:

Visiting the doctor:

Now, let's look at how changing these behaviors affects you. Go back and place a number from one to six next to each category to indicate how stressed you feel about the given adaptation. Use 1 for little to no stress and 6 for extreme stress. What did you rate as most stressful? How do you feel when you are engaging in that activity or desire to do so?

What did you rate as least stressful? Why?

_____

_____

Are you surprised about your stress level? How are you managing stress?

_____

_____

_____

_____

What behaviors do you really like having adopted? Do you imagine keeping any of them once you return home?

_____

_____

_____

_____

How would you describe your life right now in comparison to what it was like at home?

_____

_____

_____

_____

If you could choose an adjective to describe how you generally feel every day, which one would you choose? Why?

_____

_____

What do you miss about home?

_____

_____

_____

_____

Who do you miss at home? What do you miss about them?

_____

_____

How do you think this experience is changing you?

_____

_____

_____

It is common to underestimate the amount of stress that making all these changes can have on you. We want to encourage you to revisit Exercises 1 and 2, where you identified how you manage stress effectively at home, and see if you can incorporate that in your daily routine abroad. It is not unusual to experience highs and lows during your program. Strangely enough, the lows are often the times you are actually growing the most and, as we said earlier, a positive indicator that you are stepping out of your comfort zones. However, we encourage you to take time out to take care of yourself during these challenges.

EXERCISE 15: FITTING IN WHILE PURSUING PERSONAL GOALS

This exercise looks at how you are managing the balancing act between honoring your own cultural norms and choosing how to behave in order to be positively received by the host culture. In other words, how are you "fitting in"?

In the previous exercise, you identified what you have had to change. Is there anything you have purposely *not* changed? For example, some students say that even though their host family participated in religious rituals, they had no desire to adopt them even temporarily. What about you? What things do you avoid adopting?

_____

_____

_____

_____

How do you think these decisions affect how your hosts perceive you?

_____

_____

_____

_____

Obviously, there are reactions people have toward you that you may be in a position to control, while there are some reactions that you cannot change. Let's explore both.

First, let's look at how some of your choices contribute to your acceptance. In what contexts do you feel well received? For example, you may have a friendly relationship with the taxi driver who picks you up occassionally, with your host family's daughter, or with a classmate. What do you think you are doing that may contribute to this positive relationship?

_____

_____

_____

_____

_____

_____

In what contexts do you feel out of place? For example, it may seem like every time you and your American friends hang out together at a coffee shop, you feel like you're the last group to be waited on. What are you doing that may contribute to this negative situation?

_____

_____

_____

_____

Are there any situations in which you feel out of place? What behavior of yours may contribute to your separateness?

How do you know if you've done something "wrong" according to members of the host culture? What do people do or say or *not* say?

Do you have any friends from the host culture?

If not, what can you do to make some? Is this an easy thing to do, or do you experience it as a challenge?

How would you rate yourself in terms of "fitting in" using a scale of 1 to 6 (1 is feeling like you *don't* fit in, and 6 is feeling like you *do* fit in)? How do you think people from your host culture would rate you?

_____

_____

_____

_____

What did you use to evaluate yourself? For example, did you rate yourself in terms of your comfort level, the number of friends you have made, or how well you are succeeding in your classes?

_____

_____

_____

_____

_____

_____

What categories do you think the locals use to evaluate you and how you are fitting in?

_____

_____

_____

_____

_____

_____

_____

Next, let's explore this from a philosophical standpoint and look at issues that may be beyond your control. Obviously, there are no right answers to these questions. They are meant only to help you process what you are experiencing and to raise your awareness about how you might be evaluating and drawing meaning from those experiences.

Do you think it is possible for you to fully fit in as a foreigner according to how you defined it in your previous answers? Why or why not?

_____

_____

_____

_____

_____

_____

How do you feel about this reality? How does this impact your behavior?

_____

_____

_____

_____

_____

Do "foreigners" ever fit in? For example, when visitors, immigrants, exchange students, or visiting scholars come to the U.S., do they ever fully "fit in?" What standards do you think Americans use to evaluate this? Is it measured by how visitors dress, what language they speak, how much money they make, the color of their skin, and so on?

_____

_____

_____

Can you apply those same standards to your situation? If you used what you perceive Americans to use to evaluate foreigners, how would you measure up in your host country?

How do you suggest that a person balance his or her own culture with a new one? What is working for you?

_____

_____

_____

_____

How does the experience of fitting in compare with your original expectations?

_____

_____

_____

_____

_____

How are your personal goals (as identified in Exercise 2) coming along?

_____

_____

_____

_____

Learning About Your Own Culture

"Why is it difficult for Americans to understand that the first impression is what other people remember? . . . We need to remember that we represent the United States when we travel. When I was traveling the last month, I saw several cases of Americans behaving badly in public . . . I can only imagine what people were thinking—and it wasn't good."

—*Jeff*

"We'd be in

Sevilla, and there's this pack of Americans wearing
their fraternity letters, and they're speaking English
when you know that they know Spanish and that
they could interact with people. It really bugged
me. Every time I saw an American, I cringed."

—Donna

This unit is designed to help you to reflect on your sense of nationalism and whether
your experiences abroad have reshaped your perceptions of the U.S. Some students
have reported that being abroad enhanced their sense of patriotism, while other students
claimed that they viewed their country with a more critical eye. Exercise 16
asks you to explain how the U.S. is characterized by your host culture and what you
are learning about the U.S. from this experience.

EXERCISE 16: PROUD TO BE AN AMERICAN?

In what ways do locals talk about the U.S.? For example, is the U.S. mentioned in
political, social, economic, or personal contexts?

_____

_____

_____

_____

_____

_____

_____

_____

How is the U.S. characterized by the host culture? Is the U.S. revered, respected, criticized, or feared?

_____

_____

_____

_____

_____

What expectations are expressed for the U.S.? What kind of role do people think the U.S. should play in the world? How do they express these views? For example, do you see political activism? If so, is it in the newspapers, through conversation, and so on?

_____

_____

_____

_____

_____

_____

_____

_____

_____

_____

_____

_____

_____

Has anyone said anything about the U.S. that shocked or offended you? What did they say? How did you respond?

_____

_____

_____

_____

_____

_____

_____

_____

_____

_____

_____

How is the U.S. presented in the media? Does this representation seem accurate, exaggerated, or distorted?

_____

_____

_____

_____

_____

_____

What are you doing to keep up with current events in the U.S.?

How do you feel about being an American?

What insights have you developed about your country in light of engaging in discussions about it abroad?

How can you explain to people at home how the U.S. is perceived abroad?

What kind of relationship do you think the U.S. should have with your host country?

Are there things that you have learned about the U.S. that you have a desire to change?

What recommendations do you have for your fellow Americans based on the perceptions abroad?

Unit 8

Learning About Another Culture

"When I look back at that day, I see that we were looking for a party to have fun, and what we found was a celebration of the freedom that a country had enjoyed for 25 years. I will never see another event like that the rest of my life. I am happy to have been able to be there for that."

—Jeff, on his visit to another country while studying in Spain

The exercises in this unit are designed to encourage you to continue learning as much as possible about the host culture. You have a priceless opportunity now that you are living abroad to experience firsthand the kinds of things about which you have only read or heard in the past. We hope that you will decide to take us up on our suggestions but also that you will devise some of your own ways to approach cross-cultural learning. Exercise 17 invites you to update the cross-cultural research you began back in Exercise 4. In Exercise 18 we revisit the topic of journal writing now that you are living abroad. In Exercise 19, you will find a series of suggested opportunities for cross-cultural observation.

EXERCISE 17: UPDATING POLITICAL, HISTORICAL, AND CULTURAL INFORMATION ABOUT YOUR HOST SITE

As we said back when you first endeavored to answer a host of questions about your new culture before your trip, some information can be difficult to locate from the U.S. through traditional media. But now that you are living abroad, you will probably be able to fill in some gaps (or possibly correct information that was either outdated or not quite accurate). Turn back to Exercise 4 and see what changes you can make now. Keep in mind that you may need to come back to this project on several occasions as information becomes available to you throughout your stay.

EXERCISE 18: CROSS-CULTURAL OBSERVATIONS THROUGH JOURNAL WRITING

In Exercise 6, we talked a bit about the value of maintaining a journal while abroad. At that time, you were asked to consider the kinds of information that seemed appropriate for you to include in a journal while abroad. Look back at your answer. Do you still agree with your assessment? If not, how do you now envision a travel journal?

_____

_____

_____

_____

_____

Also in Exercise 6, you stated how often you thought you should write journal entries. We suggested daily, but what did you think? Have you changed your mind, or are you sticking with your original plan?

_____

_____

Restating an earlier thought, we suggest that you try to include at least one cross-cultural observation per day. *For example, you may notice small cultural differences, as did Rachel when she wrote in her journal, "The news on the TV is more graphic than in the U.S."*

Exercise 19 offers some activities that will help you observe cross-cultural differences. Each may form the basis of an entire journal entry or just a brief observation within an entry.

EXERCISE 19: CROSS-CULTURAL ACTIVITIES

Here we offer you specific activities to help you learn more about life in your host country and capitalize on the cross-cultural access that your study abroad program provides. You will notice that some of these assignments are designed to follow up on the questions raised in Exercises 4 and 17 (in which we asked you to research various aspects of your host country). All the following are activities that we suggested to our own students. Some items on the list developed out of our observations of what our students were *not* doing while abroad, and some grew out of our sense that sometimes students were not challenging themselves to think very critically about some of their cross-cultural experiences.

Using the preprinted journal pages at the end of the book, write a journal entry in response to each of these activities. You may find that along the way you come up with a few more of your own, which would be great! Similarly, as countries vary widely, a given activity that we suggest may not apply to your cross-cultural context at all or may need to be modified. For example, if we suggest that you see a domestic film in a local movie theater but there are no theaters, a reasonable adaptation might be to watch a film on television or to rent one to watch at home.

> **NOTE**
>
> If learning another language is a goal of yours (and you are completing the "Learning Another Language" units of this book), you may wish to consider doing your journal entries in the target language. Of course, you will have to be the judge as to whether your language skills at the present time will allow you to express yourself to an adequate degree. Even if you do not start out writing these entries in the target language, you may find that you are able to as your time abroad progresses.

Activity 1:   Are the meals and meal schedules what you thought they would be based on your preprogram research?

Activity 2:   Consider the programming offered on television and radio. What does it tell you about the culture and/or its values? How does this compare with the U.S.?

Activity 3:   Take a different form of transportation (hopefully one whose circuit covers parts of the city that you do not normally see). What did you see/learn that travel by your traditional means has not shown you?

Activity 4:   Go to a grocery store or market and look around at the merchandise. In what ways is this store like/unlike a typical U.S. grocery store or market in terms of merchandise, product presentation, prices, and so on? Create a reasonable weekly grocery shopping list, assuming that you are buying for just yourself. Include *all* necessities and be sure to account for main dishes, fruits, vegetables, dairy, and so on. Write the price next to each item based on the prices you encounter. Now analyze the total cost. How does it compare with what you might pay at home? How can you explain any difference?

Activity 5:   Find out how to open a bank account in your host country. Are checking and savings accounts available? Do these accounts earn interest? Do the banks allow foreigners to have accounts?

Activity 6:   Tour a museum (preferably one that you are not visiting as part of your school curriculum). It can be dedicated to art, natural history, archaeology, or any other field. Choose a particular work in the museum that interests you. Explain what the work is and why it is significant to you. Would you likely find anything similar in a museum in the U.S.?

Activity 7:   Go to the movie theater and see a nationally produced film. If possible, obtain a copy of the movie synopsis (these are sometimes available in theater lobbies) and read it carefully. What new vocabulary did you learn from reading it? Who directed the film? Who are the main actors? (Find out later from your host family or other source whether any of the principal actors are nationally famous.) What is the movie about? What did you think of it? Did the movie seem to follow a formula common in U.S. movies? If not, how did it differ? How did you react to a different formula?

Activity 8: Find out how host nationals get driver's licenses. How does the process work? Where do they learn to drive? How long does the process take? How much does it cost? How does the overall process compare to our system in the U.S.?

Activity 9: Interview a local university student about the educational system in your host country. Is the country's educational system how you thought it was based on the preprogram research you did?

Activity 10: Describe several current events in your host country using newspapers, television, and/or radio. Then cut out at least one newspaper article that represents one of these events. Summarize the article and tell how citizens seem to be reacting to this event.

Activity 11: Attend a sporting event and describe it. Does this sport exist in the U.S.? If so, are there any differences in the way it is played, viewed, and so forth? What role does this sport seem to play in the local culture?

Professional Development

"The whole thing kind of shifted right when I got off the plane, when I felt totally lost. For the first month I was still not confident talking to my own [host] family, so [imagine] going out to a perfect stranger and saying 'Let's sit down and have a business interview.' . . . Something had to change."

—Jeff, on how his professional interest project turned out differently from how he had planned it

Now that you have been living in the target culture, it is time to revisit your professional interest project. First, review your progress up to this point by answering the questions in Exercise 20. Based on your answers in this exercise, you will then be asked to think about your adaptability and problem-solving skills in Exercise 21.

EXERCISE 20: PROFESSIONAL INTEREST PROJECT: SUCCESSES AND CHALLENGES

Now that you have been living in the target culture, how is your professional interest project going?

_____

_____

_____

_____

_____

Which steps have been easy to accomplish so far? *For example, Lisa had an easy time finding museums that display Spanish pottery, so her sketching project went well*

_____

_____

_____

_____

_____

Which steps have been difficult? *For example, Jeff found it impossible to videotape businesspeople.*

_____

_____

_____

Based on your experiences what can you infer about the status of your profession in your host country? Does it exist? Is it of high prestige? Is it gender based? How does the local culture seem to relate to this profession?

_____

_____

_____

_____

_____

_____

_____

Are you considering changing any aspects of your project at this point? If so, which? Why? *For example, Lisa realized that she would have to wait until she returned to the U.S. to create Spanish-style pottery because she could not find a studio to use.*

_____

_____

_____

_____

_____

_____

How will these changes affect your ability to use the project in the future?

_____

_____

_____

_____

_____

_____

_____

_____

Has your time line for completion of this project changed?

_____

_____

_____

_____

_____

_____

_____

_____

EXERCISE 21: PROFESSIONAL ADAPTATION AND PROBLEM-SOLVING SKILLS

Adaptability and problem-solving skills are highly valued in the business, academic, and medical worlds, to name a few. Within the context of your professional interest project, what can you say at this point about your own ability to adapt to unfamiliar circumstances?

_____

_____

_____

_____

_____

_____

Can you identify specific ways in which you have applied creative problem-solving skills in the execution of your project?

_____

_____

_____

_____

_____

_____

_____

Learning Another Language

"After learning [Spanish] in junior high and high school and college, it finally came together. As I was relearning it, I was actually using it. I got so good there. I was so proud. I wasn't perfect, but I got good."

—Donna

"For the first

time I walked down the street alone. I walked from the university (a part of it I had never seen before) to my apartment (I took the metro). It's a bit strange walking in a big group of students when everybody knows the language except me. But it's interesting too."

—Rachel

"The first

time I traveled by myself was when I went to Granada. . . . I met this guy, and we talked for like three hours. I understood everything he said. That was the first time I was thrown into a situation because I wasn't with any-one who could speak English. And it was really cool!"

—Beth

This unit will help you begin your language-learning journal and ask you to revisit both your language-learning goals and the ideas you had for keeping on track.

EXERCISE 22: LANGUAGE JOURNAL

If you did not already do so during Exercise 12, it is now time to begin your language-learning journal. Because your time is precious, we suggest that this not take the form of a completely different journal from the one described in Exercise 18. You will notice in the preprinted journal pages at the end of the book that language-learning issues have been integrated with cultural learning and personal observations.

Consider the following types of content for the language portion of your journal.

1. Copy down interesting new words that you hear in classes throughout the day as well as their definitions. *For example, Lisa wrote in the margins of her journal such items as the following:*

   me quedo muerto = speechless
   rezar = to pray
   cesto = large basket

   Take advantage of all the opportunities available to you for language learning. *For example, Jill wrote in her journal that she liked going to the gym for several reasons, one of which was practicing her Spanish and learning new words—after which she announced that she had just learned the word "estirar," which means "to stretch."*

2. Chronicle your language-learning development, noting milestones (e.g., the first time you actually understand directions given to you by a native speaker on the street) and setbacks (e.g., days when you can't seem to get out one linguistically correct sentence). While the former are obviously the kinds of things you will want to remember for posterity (and a little self-confidence boost!), the latter will be of value, too. It is often the challenging moment that helps us grow. Keeping a record of the tough times will allow you to look back later and be proud of the difficulties you overcame.

3. If you travel, write down vocabulary that seems to be regional/local. If you have the opportunity, ask locals if these words or terms are indeed specific to the region. When you return home to your study site, share them with host family members, course instructors, or other individuals and see if they can add any interesting details to your investigation. This new vocabulary and background information will not only serve to increase your vocabulary in general but may also serve as the foundation for a project in a language course on your return home. A U.S. English-language example of this activity would be to copy down different regional terms for a given item. For example, what southerners in the U.S. tend to call a *bag* midwesterners may call a *sack*. What southerners often call a *soft drink* some midwesterners call a *soda* and still others refer to as a *pop*.

4. Pick a particular grammar point as your focus for a given day or even week and pay attention to how it is evidenced in what you hear and see on the streets, in advertisements, in music, on television, or from teachers, host family members, or friends. Remember that you will have almost constant access to "live grammar," something that is not available to most of us while we study the foreign language in our home country. Use this resource to your advantage. Test

out hypotheses about how this grammar point works and ask people. Most people are glad to see that you are interested in their language. For example, if you are trying to figure out the appropriate uses of the subjunctive, listen to your instructors' speech as well as that of other native speakers. As you listen to music on the radio or perhaps watch music videos, listen for more examples of the subjunctive in action. From all the examples you hear, you should be able to refine your understanding of when to use it.

..... You're going

home . . .
But before you go, be sure to read ahead and
complete the first part of Exercise 23.

Personal Development

"Re-entry shock was terrible for me. I hated it here for a really long time.... My family——we never fight.... I was yelling at my mom for no reason at all. She'd be like, 'I understand that you feel weird,' and I'd just yell and start crying——it was bad, really bad."

—*Samantha*

"To other

people it was a trip. Like 'How was your trip?'
For me it was this whole section of my life.
It was my life for three or four months."

—Donna

This unit explores the process of fitting back into the environment you left behind during your study abroad experience. Many of our students report being personally changed by the study abroad experience. Reactions range from feeling more capable of being independent to having fundamentally changed beliefs and behaviors. We hope the exercises thus far have made you mindful of your growth and have somewhat prepared you for the final phase of this experience——going home.

Exercise 23 is divided into two parts. The first part you complete immediately prior to going home. It asks you to evaluate how you have (or have not) attained the personal goals you established in Exercise 2. It also asks you to begin thinking about how you might deal with family and friends who will be anxious to hear about your adventures.

The second part of Exercise 23 should be completed after you've arrived home. It asks you to evaluate your new (but old) environment and what you might be missing from your other "home" abroad.

Finally, Exercise 24 encourages you to think about ways of maintaining some traditions you enjoyed while abroad and to identify obstacles you might be encountering as you attempt to fit this new self into your old environment.

EXERCISE 23: FITTING YOUR NEW SELF INTO AN OLD ENVIRONMENT: COPING WITH RE-ENTRY SHOCK

Let's revisit the goals you articulated in Exercise 2. Refer to them as needed while you're answering the following questions.

Which goals did you achieve that made the most impact on you?

_____

_____

_____

_____

If you had known then what you know now, would your goals have been different? What would they have been?

_____

_____

_____

_____

Which goals did you not accomplish? Why?

_____

_____

_____

_____

What did you accomplish or experience that you never expected to?

_____

_____

_____

_____

If you could do it all over again, what would you change about your experience abroad?

_____

_____

_____

_____

Let's think about the life you've been away from while abroad. With whom have you been keeping in contact?

_____

_____

_____

_____

_____

How have their lives been different while you've been away?

_____

_____

_____

_____

How do you think they are feeling about your coming home?

_____

_____

_____

_____

How are you feeling about seeing them and being part of their lives again?

_____

_____

_____

_____

How do you imagine it will be to get reacquainted now that you've been away?

_____

_____

_____

_____

How do you think your family and friends think *you* have changed? Do you think they are expecting any differences in your behavior or worldview?

_____

_____

_____

_____

_____

How do *you* think you've changed?

_____

_____

_____

_____

_____

How do you think *they* might have changed during your absence?

_____

_____

_____

_____

_____

What challenges do you anticipate once you get home? For example, some students say it was really difficult to have a curfew from parents when they have had the freedom to travel the world on their own schedule. What adjustments are you expecting?

_____

_____

_____

_____

Is there anything (such as a cultural tradition, or even a fast-food restaurant) that you are particularly excited to get home to?

_____

_____

_____

_____

What do you think you are going to miss about your home abroad?

_____

_____

_____

_____

_____

Do you have any plans for how you are going to say good-bye to people?

_____

_____

_____

_____

Do you feel particularly appreciative toward any locals? Do you have any ideas about how to express that gratitude?

_____

_____

_____

_____

With whom do you think you'll keep in touch when you return home, and how do you imagine doing this?

_____

_____

_____

_____

_____

_____

_____

NOTE

It would be a good idea to look at Appendix 3 now and begin to fill in contact information for new friends, professional contacts, and so on. We encourage you to compile this information sooner rather than later, as sometimes you think you will see someone before you leave, and then the opportunity never arises.

Complete this next section when you have been home for about a week.

What *do* you like about your "new" environment?

_____

_____

_____

_____

What *don't* you like about your new environment?

_____

_____

_____

_____

Were there any immediate impressions you had within the first few hours of your arrival (e.g., some people noticed how wide the streets seemed)?

_____

_____

_____

_____

How are you spending your time now? How does that differ from when you were abroad?

_____

_____

_____

_____

_____

How are you feeling about being at home?

_____

_____

_____

_____

_____

_____

How do you experience your family and friends now that you're back? Were you able to get reacquainted like you thought?

_____

_____

_____

_____

_____

What relationships are most challenging? Why?

_____

_____

_____

_____

_____

_____

_____

Are you aware of any other ways you've changed or grown now that you've been home for a little while?

_____

_____

_____

_____

_____

When you look back at the exercises you completed in the previous units, does reentering the U.S. feel similar to what you experienced when you went abroad? Think back to Exercises 13, 14, and 15 on being a foreigner, culture shock, and fitting in; what parallels do you see with coming home?

_____

_____

_____

_____

_____

_____

_____

_____

_____

_____

_____

It's important to note that most students experience an adjustment period when they come home. Although it's temporary, it does take some time to get reacquainted with your old life, often using a new perspective. Students who have experienced significant growth and change sometimes have to adjust their original social networks and pursue different interests than they did before they went abroad to feel more comfortable. We encourage you to keep the study abroad spirit alive by adopting a sense of exploration back home. Who knows what you had been missing because you weren't looking!

EXERCISE 24: MAINTAINING TRADITIONS FROM YOUR EXPERIENCE

This exercise encourages you to look at lifestyle changes you adopted abroad that served you well and to see if and how you could integrate those personal changes back home.

If you look back at how you had to change your behavior while abroad (Exercise 14), were there some lifestyle changes that served you? For example, some students had to change their diet while abroad and realized how much better they felt without red meat. What about you?

_____

_____

_____

_____

_____

Are you able to maintain some of those behaviors at home? For example, some students had to walk a lot more, as they didn't have a car at their disposal and really enjoyed the extra exercise. They were able to incorporate this into their lives back home by walking to class or work or just making a point to walk for the sake of walking.

_____

_____

_____

_____

_____

What obstacles do you face trying to integrate these rituals into your life back home? Are there ways of overcoming them?

_____

_____

_____

_____

_____

_____

_____

What do you miss about your "other home"?

_____

_____

_____

_____

_____

Are you interested in going back?

_____

_____

_____

_____

Learning About Your Own Culture

"We have so many things that we don't need. I come back and have this whole room full of stuff . . . I don't need that! The Europeans I knew didn't have as much stuff as we did."

—Samantha

"How the

people drive their cars [in the U.S.]—it drives me
insane! I don't want to get in the car to go to
the gas station just to buy a pack of cigarettes.
I was like, 'We can walk. We live down the street!'"

—*Lisa*

This unit encourages you to consider how you might use what you have learned
about the U.S. Having witnessed a different lifestyle abroad and gaining insight into
how the U.S. is perceived from abroad, we want you to explore how your wisdom
could be shared with others. This is one of the many benefits of study abroad programs, as students are in a position of acquiring substantial information that they can
bring back and share with their communities at home. Exercise 25 asks you to think
about how you are going to share your experiences, with particular attention to what
you have learned about the U.S.

EXERCISE 25: REMINISCING, SHARING, AND EDUCATING OTHERS

In Exercise 16, you identified how the U.S. was perceived by your host culture. What
recommendations did you have for your fellow Americans based on the perceptions
abroad?

_____

_____

_____

_____

_____

_____

_____

Do those recommendations still make sense to you? Have you thought of any others?

_____

_____

_____

_____

_____

_____

_____

_____

_____

_____

_____

_____

_____

_____

_____

_____

_____

_____

_____

_____

_____

How and where could you communicate these recommendations? Would you consider political and/or social activism as a means of sharing what you have learned?

_____

_____

_____

_____

_____

_____

_____

What organizations might support your cause?

_____

_____

_____

_____

_____

_____

_____

_____

_____

_____

_____

_____

_____

How have your perceptions about your country changed now that you have completed your study abroad experience?

_____

_____

_____

_____

_____

_____

_____

_____

_____

_____

_____

_____

_____

_____

_____

What other experiences could you pursue to continue learning about the U.S. and how Americans relate to people throughout the world?

_____

_____

_____

_____

_____

_____

_____

Unit 13

Learning About Another Culture

"I liked the journal. It helps me to remember little things which would not be remembered otherwise."

—Samantha

Now that you have returned, there are many things you can do to keep yourself involved in the cross-cultural learning process. In this unit, we suggest specific ways to do just that. First, in Exercise 26, you will take one more look at the information you gathered about your host culture. Exercises 27 through 29 provide an opportunity for you to select key information from your journal for further consideration. In Exercise 30, we offer several suggestions to keep your international experience going and to share what you have learned with others.

EXERCISE 26: A FINAL LOOK AT POLITICAL, HISTORICAL, AND CULTURAL INFORMATION ABOUT YOUR HOST SITE

Believe it or not, we are going to ask you to look back at the information you collected first in Exercise 4 and updated in Exercise 17. You may be asking, "What more could you possibly expect me to do with this information?" We have several ideas in mind. First, make sure that the information is correct. Is there anything that you need to change at this point?

Second, have you been able to answer all the questions? If so, great! If not, why do you think that is? Can you think of any culturally based reason why not?

_____

_____

_____

_____

Third, look at each category and ask yourself what other questions you would now be able to answer had they been asked. Or for that matter, are there entire categories of cultural information we did not include that you could have talked about? _For example, Jill could now write about various regional dances of Spain, and Andrea could write about advertising practices._

Now that you have analyzed the categories you wrote (or could have written) about, are you surprised at how much you have learned? At what you have been unable to learn?

_____

_____

_____

_____

We hope that if you chose to do this exercise in each unit, you are now feeling a great sense of accomplishment. You've earned it. (If you did not do the exercise, it's still not too late! Just go back to Exercise 4 and use it as a quiz to see how much you learned about your host culture while abroad or as an organizing principle for future research!)

Looking back at your answers, do you find that there are certain categories about which you learned quite a bit more than others? Why is that? That is, are these topics in which you have always been more interested, has your experience abroad spawned a new area of interest for you, or was the information simply more readily available? This is an interesting issue to ponder and one that might help you identify specific avenues for further research.

_____

_____

_____

_____

_____

Finally, try to envision doing something with all this information you have gathered, such as giving a talk to a related class at school or creating a Web site.

_____

_____

_____

_____

_____

_____

_____

Introduction to Exercises 27 to 29: "A Private Journal Critique." If you kept a cross-cultural journal while you were abroad (even sporadically), it is time to look back at it now but in a new way. Most of the time when we reread a journal, we simply read through it and reminisce about the memories it conjures up. These activities will be different, and we hope that they will help you develop a "big-picture" sense of what you accomplished while abroad.

EXERCISE 27: A PRIVATE JOURNAL CRITIQUE—
WHAT DID YOU STUDY?

In Exercise 26, we asked you to analyze your learning about topics we provided. In Exercise 27, you will identify which aspects of the target culture most caught your attention while you were abroad and analyze any sort of pattern formed. After doing so, consider whether any might be avenues for further study now that you are home.

The following presents one way of analyzing your journal for cross-cultural content, but feel free to do this any way you wish.

1. Using a highlighter, read through each journal entry and mark any information that relates to the target culture.

2. Next to each highlighted block, write the topic (such as food, politics, fashion, and so on) that the section of text reflects.

3. Using the list provided (and adding other topics as needed), put a mark next to a topic each time it is mentioned in your journal.

4. Once you have completed the process for the entire journal, go back and count up the marks.

The topics list that follows (Dowell, 1996) breaks down possible cultural information across four broad categories. Possible topics are listed under each, but feel free to add more topics in the blank spaces provided in order to reflect your journal contents.

Environmental

Natural

_____ Topography
_____ Flora/Fauna
_____ Weather
_____
_____

Man-Made

_____ Architecture
_____ States/Cities
_____ Attractions
_____ Art
_____ Pollution
_____ Urban/Rural Settings
_____

Intrapersonal

Personal Needs

_____ Food
_____ Clothing
_____ Housing
_____
_____

Beliefs

_____ Priorities
_____ Time
_____ Money
_____ Religion
_____

Dowell, Michele-Marie. (1996). *Perspectives toward the Target Culture by Selected Participants in a Study Abroad Program in Mexico.* Unpublished dissertation.

Interpersonal (Public)

_____ Government
_____ Transportation
_____ Economy
_____ Leisure Activities
_____ Traditions
_____ Social Issues
_____
_____

Interpersonal (Private)

_____ Family
_____ Gender Roles
_____ Friendships
_____ Ethnic Background
_____
_____

Now it's time to analyze your findings using the following questions as a point of departure.

1. Which topics were most popular in your journal?

_____

_____

_____

_____

2. Does this surprise you? Why or why not?

_____

_____

_____

_____

3. Does this tally by topic suggest an area of interest for further study?

_____

_____

_____

_____

4. Are there aspects of the culture that you would have thought would be more prominently represented in your journal?

_____

_____

_____

_____

5. If so, might you now go back and research these aspects further?

_____

_____

_____

_____

EXERCISE 28: A PRIVATE JOURNAL CRITIQUE—WHERE DID PROBLEMS ARISE?

Travel is like daily life in that there will always be good and bad moments. It is unrealistic to expect that no problems will arise during the course of a study abroad program. In this exercise, you will be asked to identify a few of the "frustrating moments" that you experienced while abroad as captured in your journal. For each, consider the following questions:

1. What was the frustration? Create a title for it as if it were going to be the title of a short story.

   TITLE: _____

2. Was the issue resolved (either at the time of the journal entry or later on in the study abroad experience)?

_____

_____

_____

3. If so, how did you manage to resolve it?

_____

_____

_____

_____

_____

4. If you never did resolve it to your satisfaction, could you do so now? How might you go about that?

_____

_____

_____

_____

_____

5. In any case, how has this experience contributed to your perception of the host culture?

_____

_____

_____

_____

_____

_____

_____

EXERCISE 29: A PRIVATE JOURNAL CRITIQUE—CONTEXTS OF COMMUNICATION

Back to the old "what you say and how you say it" issue. As you have just reviewed the contents of your journal and reminisced about what you learned and how you reacted to elements of your host culture, it is time to consider the contexts of communication in which you now find yourself. When talking with your close friends or family, it is natural to share your most basic reactions without editing or otherwise filtering your comments very much. On the other hand, when you sense that you are serving as a student ambassador, you may automatically be more mindful about how you educate people about differences. That said, we would like for you to think about three issues.

1. What do you think your role should be at this point? Is it your job to educate others about cross-cultural differences relating to your host culture? If your answer is yes, how will you go about sharing your insights in a positive manner?

_____

_____

_____

_____

_____

2. In daily life we often do not need to filter our comments to those around us because they have access to the culture and can easily form their own impressions. However, most people will not have spent extensive time in the host culture from which you just returned. So the question is: How do you balance a desire to be candid in conversations with friends and family with your role as an ambassador for your host culture?

_____

_____

_____

_____

_____

3. If you are interested in making it clear to your audience (be it family, friends, or others) that you are referring to your own interpretation about the host culture rather than citing facts, how might you do that? We can suggest prefacing statements with phrases such as "In my opinion . . ." and "I thought that . . .". What ideas do you have?

_____

_____

_____

_____

EXERCISE 30: STAYING INTERNATIONALIZED AND SHARING YOUR EXPERIENCES WITH OTHERS

There are many ways to keep learning about the culture from which you just returned as well as others with which you are not yet familiar. Following are several of our ideas, after which we will ask that you identify any ideas you can add to our list.

1. If you are still in school and have not already done so, take courses in such fields as history, political science, anthropology, communications, or foreign language (perhaps studying a language other than the one you used abroad). Such courses may or may not have interested you before your experience abroad, but now you would be experiencing them from a new perspective.

2. Join a club or organization dedicated to learning more about (or interacting with) different cultures.

3. Offer to give a presentation to a class, club, or organization at your college or university or in the community. In the presentation, share your insights as well as pictures and other memorabilia from your trip. You may be surprised by how many people will be intrigued by your experience.

What ideas can you add to our list?

_____

_____

_____

_____

_____

_____

_____

_____

Unit 14

Professional Development

"My kitchen

manager where I work always likes to try new things. So I'm going to give him some recipes [from Spain]. If they turn out, I'll see if they can be another entry on our menu."

—Beth, on the possible application of her professional interest project on restaurant management in Spain to her current job working in a Hispanic restaurant

In Exercise 31, you will be asked to reconsider the professional goals you established for your study abroad experience. Exercise 32 offers an opportunity to assess the professional interest project you completed, and Exercise 33 provides ways in which to make your professional growth known to others.

EXERCISE 31: PROFESSIONAL GOALS ATTAINMENT

Look back at the professional goals you set in Exercise 7 and sought to attain while abroad. Are you satisfied with your results? If so, that's great. If not, is there anything you can do now to reach them? (Remember that such sources as the Internet may offer opportunities for further research.)

_____

_____

_____

_____

_____

_____

_____

_____

EXERCISE 32: CRITICALLY EXAMINING YOUR PROFESSIONAL INTEREST PROJECT

Think about your professional interest project and what you learned from it by answering the following questions. You may notice that several questions are similar to those asked in Exercise 20, and that is because we anticipate that other developments may have occurred in your project since you completed that exercise.

Which aspects of the project ended up being easiest to accomplish? Why do you think they were easy?

_____

_____

_____

_____

Did the aspects of the project you identified as difficult in Exercise 20 continue to be challenging? How did you handle the situation(s)?

If you changed any aspects of the project while abroad, were the changes helpful?

Looking back on the entire experience, did you learn more about the status of your profession in your host country and how the local culture relates to this profession?

_____

_____

_____

_____

_____

_____

What do you think of the finished product? Of which aspects of your professional interest project are you particularly proud?

_____

_____

_____

_____

_____

_____

_____

_____

EPILOGUE TO EXERCISE 32

We thought that after following our students' progress throughout the units on professional development, you might like to know how Jeff's and Lisa's professional interest projects turned out. Jeff ended up writing a paper on Spanish business practices in Spain. While he was not able to videotape the various interviews, he took good notes. He incorporated the questions and answers from his business interviews into his course paper. He also wrote about the use of the Internet and the concept of owning one's own business.

Along with a formal paper, Lisa produced a book of color sketches of the styles of pottery found throughout Spain. In the book, she also included photographs of the local artist she interviewed. As part of the lesson plan she created to use in teaching a lesson to local children, Lisa made several large two-dimensional cardboard versions of several pottery designs. She ended up teaching her lesson to the children over a series of Saturdays.

EXERCISE 33: USING YOUR PROFESSIONAL INTEREST PROJECT WITHIN A PROFESSIONAL NETWORK

You have invested a great deal of time and energy in your professional interest project. It is important that you now ensure that your work be noticed by potential employers. Consider the following:

How will you describe your professional interest project on your résumé?

Can you think of new local audiences with whom to share the results of your project (as compared with your list in Exercise 9)?

How might you make your project available to a broader audience (e.g., publishing an article in a travel or professional journal or creating a Web page)?

_____

_____

_____

_____

_____

What steps can you now take to continue your professional development as it relates to your recent study abroad experience? For example, if you have one or two more years in school before graduating, can you become involved in organizations or enroll in courses that might be useful?

_____

_____

_____

_____

_____

_____

_____

Unit 15

Learning Another Language

"Learning Spanish is just the best thing I've ever done. I've used it so much being back here.... I got a job for four days after getting back and was working in a kitchen at a golf tournament with all these Mexicans. And I was just in *heaven* speaking Spanish every minute for like 10 hours a day there. They were like, 'Why are you speaking Spanish with an accent from Spain?' And I was like, 'Wow, I picked one up!'"

—*Lisa*

"I know

I need to use [Spanish] in my career down the line,
but it's this gap right here that I am not using
it that I need to keep it up."

—Donna

In this unit, we focus on the maintenance and further development of the language skills you gained while abroad. If you did not advance as much as you had hoped, now is as good a time as any to rededicate yourself to this endeavor. In Exercise 34, you are encouraged to organize what you learned about the language while abroad. In Exercise 35, we suggest ways to maintain and further develop your skills. And in Exercise 36, we ask you to consider ways in which you might share what you have learned with others.

EXERCISE 34: CREATING A LANGUAGE RESOURCE

There are two steps to this exercise, the first dealing with organizing the language portion of your journal and the second requiring a revisiting of key aspects of it.

Step 1: Go back through the notes you jotted in the language portion of your journal and organize the information by topic in another place (a spiral notebook, on your computer, and so on). Topics might include formal vocabulary, regional vocabulary, slang, specific grammar points, regional accents, and so forth. This organization process will make the information more accessible to you in the future as you continue learning the language.

Step 2: Look through your language journal entries for times you said you did not understand a given aspect (typically a grammar point) of the target language. In each case, ask yourself, "Do I understand this now?" If so, wonderful! If not, why not research it further? For example, if you said that you were having a hard time understanding the subjunctive (after all, it is not used much in American English), have you made sense of it yet? If not, you could use your journal notes as a point of departure and ask a professor for an explanation of this grammar point.

EXERCISE 35: MAINTAINING AND FURTHER DEVELOPING YOUR LANGUAGE SKILLS

The following represent several ideas to help you not only maintain the skills you have worked hard to develop but also continue the development process. This is by no means an exhaustive list, so we encourage you to identify other activities that might work for you.

1. If there are language tables at your school for those who wish to practice their speaking and listening skills, make a commitment to participate on a regular basis.

2. If there is not such a program available, be the person to organize one!

3. Locate a community of native speakers where you live and seek opportunities to become involved in activities there.

4. Commit yourself to corresponding (in the target language) with your host family and/or friends abroad. The key here is to do so on some sort of a regular basis!

Can you think of other activities that will help you maintain your use of the language? List your ideas here.

_____

_____

_____

_____

_____

_____

EXERCISE 36: SHARING YOUR LANGUAGE LEARNING WITH OTHERS

As in Exercise 35, we offer just a few ideas to get you started, confident in the knowledge that you will be able to think of other activities that suit your particular situation. You may notice that the first of these suggestions overlaps with one offered in Exercise 30. The difference is that in that exercise we were focusing on the sharing of cross-cultural learning, whereas here we wish to help you identify ways to share with others the language skills that you have learned.

1. Consider offering to give a presentation (in the foreign language) on your host country to appropriate-level language classes or clubs at your college or university or in a local high school or middle school. Be sure to take along some of the memorabilia you brought back from your host country. Not only will your audience

enjoy seeing such items as postcards, photos, coins, and other realia, but reference to these items during the presentation will help your audience understand you. (This is particularly true if you present to beginning or intermediate-level groups.)

2. Offer your services as a language tutor at either your own or any of the local schools mentioned previously.

3. If your language skills are advanced enough, offer to volunteer as an interpreter at the local hospital or court. If your community is home to a population of native speakers, there may be an occasional need for interpreters.

Can you think of any other ways to share your language learning with others? If so, list them here.

_____

_____

_____

_____

_____

_____

Congratulations

on completing your journey!
We hope it serves as a stepping
stone for future adventures.

Implementation Tips for the Study Abroad Administrator/ Faculty Director

Although there is no "right" way to incorporate this workbook into existing orientations or study abroad classes, we want to provide a few models to illustrate its versatility. We describe these options from least labor intensive to most.

I. **The self-directed approach:** This is where the study abroad administrator requires students to purchase the textbook independently (or you could collect a fee with the other program fees and order it bulk rate) to ensure that all study abroad participants receive it. A note in the acceptance letter or within the orientation materials that endorses the completion of this textbook is all you would need to provide this opportunity to your students. By doing so, you could offer them (with little effort on your part) guidance about how to approach, experience, and process their study abroad experience.

II. **The orientation enhancer:** As in the self-directed approach, the study abroad administrator requires students to purchase the text and endorses its completion. In addition, targeted units of the text are incorporated into existing orientation formats. For example, if you meet with students two or three times before they go abroad, why not assign certain units within the predeparture phase to be completed for a meeting and then simply dedicate some time (as little as a half hour) within the "normal" agenda to discuss targeted questions as a group? If you have a re-entry program (or need a convenient resource to start one!), you might also use this as a tool to guide re-entry discussions, again by encouraging students to complete targeted units before a meeting, or even use the meeting for completing the exercises as a group. Furthermore, the professional interest projects students complete on-site could be shared in a symposium on their return. This symposium could serve a dual purpose. First, it would help students process their accomplishment and find applications for their experience back at home. Second, this same public forum could be a wonderful recruitment tool, providing future students with a way to learn how study abroad has professional relevance and what personal impact it can have on people.

III. **Faculty-led short-term programs—the small-group approach:** Faculty who take students on study abroad programs have a ready-made lesson plan using this textbook that requires no additional teaching resources, except the motivation to listen and review students' projects. Using the suggested time line this book provides as a guide, simply create your own time line (similar to one you would create in a syllabus) that tells students what days certain units will be discussed so they are prepared. (For shorter programs, you may need to be more selective, which means you will not formally review every unit.) Then, whether you meet daily or weekly, use the questions outlined in the textbook to provide the agenda for each meeting. You can even put students into groups and then have a spokesperson share the highlights/conclusions drawn from their discussion. The textbook does the work. All you need to do is be a strong advocate for critical thinking skills and independent exploration. If you have an expertise that supplements students' personal discovery, feel free to share that information as well. You may also find the results of the discussion a convenient means of assessing where students could use a tutorial or what lecture topics might be of interest. Grading can be based on completeness and thoroughness of exercises (omitting the more personal sections), students' professional interest projects, and their participation in discussion.

IV. **The study abroad class:** This is really the most labor intensive means of covering every unit formally with students over a regularly scheduled period of time. Although this is time consuming, we found it to be very rewarding both to the students and to us. Our class met for two to three hours, five times prior to departure and four times on re-entry. Students were expected to work independently while completing the on-site activities and exercises and their personal interest project. This workbook can serve as the foundation for a course, or it can complement and/or supplement activities, lectures, and other classroom rituals that already exist. If language learning is a goal, you may wish to do what we did, which was to have at least part of each class meeting carried out in the target language. Students in our class earned credit for three one-hour courses using an interdisciplinary studies lower-level course number designation. Grading was based on completeness and thoroughness of exercises (many of which we put into this textbook), students' professional interest projects, and their participation in classroom discussions.

Appendix 2

My Contact Information Abroad

This book belongs to:

If found, please contact:

Travel Itinerary:

Departure date: Airline   Flight number   Airport   Departure time

Arrival date and time:

Contact Information:

Host family name or name of residence:

Phone number:

How to make a phone call from the U.S.:

International operator   Country code   City code   Phone number

How to make a call when I'm abroad:

International operator   Country code   City code   Phone number

Host school:

International student adviser/program contact person abroad:

Name:
Address:
Phone number:
E-mail:

Study abroad adviser/program contact person at home:

Name:
Address:
Phone number:
E-mail:
24 hour contact number (i.e., college/university police):

In Case of Emergency:

Contact information for nearest U.S. Embassy:

Contact information for nearest clinic/hospital:

Notes:

Appendix 3

Address Book

People I want to keep in touch with at home while I'm studying abroad:

Name: _____

Address:

    Local: _____

    _____

    Permanent: _____

    _____

Phone number: _____

E-mail address: _____

Name: _____

Address:

    Local: _____

    _____

    Permanent: _____

    _____

Phone number: _____

E-mail address: _____

Name: _____

Address:

    Local: _____

    _____

    Permanent: _____

    _____

Phone number: _____

E-mail address: _____

Name: _____

Address:

    Local: _____

_____

    Permanent: _____

_____

Phone number: _____

E-mail address: _____

Name: _____

Address:

    Local: _____

_____

    Permanent: _____

_____

Phone number: _____

E-mail address: _____

Name: _____

Address:

    Local: _____

_____

    Permanent: _____

_____

Phone number: _____

E-mail address: _____

Name: _____

Address:

    Local: _____

    _____

    Permanent: _____

    _____

    _____

Phone number: _____

E-mail address: _____

Name: _____

Address:

    Local: _____

    _____

    Permanent: _____

    _____

Phone number: _____

E-mail address: _____

Name: _____

Address:

    Local: _____

    _____

    Permanent: _____

    _____

Phone number: _____

E-mail address: _____

Name: _____

Address:

     Local: _____

     _____

     Permanent: _____

     _____

     _____

Phone number: _____

E-mail address: _____

Name: _____

Address:

     Local: _____

     _____

     Permanent: _____

     _____

     _____

Phone number: _____

E-mail address: _____

Name: _____

Address:

     Local: _____

     _____

     Permanent: _____

     _____

     _____

Phone number: _____

E-mail address: _____

Name: _____

Address:

     Local: _____

     _____

     Permanent: _____

     _____

Phone number: _____

E-mail address: _____

Name: _____

Address:

     Local: _____

     _____

     Permanent: _____

     _____

Phone number: _____

E-mail address: _____

Name: _____

Address:

     Local: _____

     _____

     Permanent: _____

     _____

Phone number: _____

E-mail address: _____

Name: _____

Address:

    Local: _____

    _____

    Permanent: _____

    _____

Phone number: _____

E-mail address: _____

Name: _____

Address:

    Local: _____

    _____

    Permanent: _____

    _____

Phone number: _____

E-mail address: _____

Name: _____

Address:

    Local: _____

    _____

    Permanent: _____

    _____

Phone number: _____

E-mail address: _____

International friends I want to keep in touch with when I return home:

Name: _____

Address:

    Local: _____

    _____

    Permanent:

    _____

    _____

Phone number: _____

E-mail address: _____

Name: _____

Address:

    Local: _____

    _____

    Permanent:

    _____

    _____

Phone number: _____

E-mail address: _____

Name: _____

Address:

    Local: _____

Permanent: _____

_____

_____

Phone number: _____

E-mail address: _____

Name: _____

Address:

Local: _____

_____

Permanent: _____

_____

_____

Phone number: _____

E-mail address: _____

Name: _____

Address:

Local: _____

_____

Permanent: _____

_____

_____

Phone number: _____

E-mail address: _____

Name: _____

Address:

Local: _____

Permanent:

Phone number: _____

E-mail address: _____

Name: _____

Address:

     Local: _____

     _____

     Permanent: _____

     _____

     _____

Phone number: _____

E-mail address: _____

Name: _____

Address:

     Local: _____

     _____

     Permanent: _____

     _____

     _____

Phone number: _____

E-mail address: _____

Name: _____

Address:

     Local: _____

     _____

     Permanent: _____

     _____

     _____

Phone number: _____

E-mail address: _____

Appendix 4

Packing List

What is the weather going to be like when you are abroad?

How much luggage do the airlines permit you to check, and how much can you take on board?

How much can you reasonably carry by yourself? What forms of transportation will you be taking, and how much room will you have on these vehicles to maneuver large bags?

How will you care for your clothes abroad? Are there dry-cleaning conveniences? How much does that cost? Will you have access to a washer and dryer and/or to an iron?

How much walking will you be doing on a daily basis?

Do you have to dress professionally for any occasions?

Are there any customs in your host culture that will affect your choice of clothing (e.g., women's heads may need to be covered in places of worship)?

What electric voltage do they use in your host country? Will you need to take an adapter and/or converter with you?

How much space do you think you will have to store your personal belongings?

Here is a list of packing categories that we encourage you to consider. We have left space to let you fill in the specific items within each category.

TOILETRIES:

MEDICATION: Will you have enough prescription medication for the duration of your trip, or will you need to get it refilled while abroad? What is the generic name for each prescription medicine?

FOOTWEAR:

CASUAL WEAR:

FORMAL WEAR:

ALL WEATHER GEAR:

MEMORABILIA SUPPLIES (e.g., film, camera):

SCHOOL SUPPLIES:

PERSONAL ITEMS (e.g., phone card, leisure items):

OTHER:

Appendix 5

Money Matters

Here is an open budget that we encourage you to complete so you understand your financial responsibilities before you go abroad and while you are there. This will also help you determine what forms of money you need to consider taking abroad.

Tuition/instructional costs at your host school: $ _____

Tuition and fees at your home school: $ _____

Room: $ _____

Food: $ _____

Utilities: $ _____

Administrative fees: $ _____

Books/school supplies: $ _____

Airfare: $ _____

Local transportation costs (e.g., metro passes): $ _____

Personal expenses: $ _____

Additional money for travel: $ _____

Total Estimated Expenses: $ _____

Which of the estimated expenses are you paying to your school or study abroad organization before you go?

Which expenses will you have to pay while you're abroad?

Are you using financial aid to pay for your expenses? Will you receive your money on time? Have you checked that all types of your aid can be used for this experience?

How will you get money while abroad? Will your ATM card be effective internationally? Will there be additional charges to use it abroad?

Would traveler's checks be useful? Would it be worthwhile to open a bank account while abroad? Do you have a credit card?

If you have a financial crisis while abroad, how can you get more money quickly? Do you have people at home who can put money in your bank account?

What is the exchange rate for currency in your host country?

How much does it cost for daily necessities abroad? What kind of budget will you give yourself each week?

Appendix 6

Taking Care of Personal Business

Before you leave, you will need to make arrangements to attend to some personal matters that will require attention in your absence. Here are some issues to consider so you can plan accordingly.

Academic issues

How will you register for classes for the semester you are returning from study abroad?

Do you know what the procedures are for earning the kind of academic credit you desire for your study abroad experience?

Do the grades you earn abroad count toward your GPA?

Will you have to be readmitted once you return to your home institution?

Financial issues

Have you signed all your financial aid documents?

Do you have any credit card bills, student loan payments, or any other financial obligations that need to be attended to while you're abroad? Who is going to take care of these things?

Communication

Where will mail from school, work, and other places be sent while you are abroad? What kind of arrangements do you need to make to facilitate this process?

How will family and friends maintain contact with you while abroad? Will you get a cell phone, e-mail, or write?

Does your home institution know you will be away for a semester? (This pertains to students not using a program through their home school.) Have you talked to a study abroad adviser about this decision?

Housing

What do you have to do before leaving to get out of any housing contracts, leases, or roommate obligations?

Where are you planning to live when you return? What do you have to do before you leave or while abroad in order to secure your future housing?

Other issues

Extracurricular Travel Plans

This is a template for the things you might consider when making additional travel plans while abroad. Traveling is one of the highlights of the study abroad experience, but like other things, it requires careful planning.

Destination: Date:

What kind of transportation will you use to get there?

What travel times are available? Do you have to buy your tickets in advance, or can you wait until the day of travel?

How long does it take to travel from your host site to this destination?

How many days would you like to stay there?

What accommodations are available, and what times can you arrive and depart from them? Do they require a reservation in advance, or can you reserve a room on the day of your arrival?

What sites do you want to see while you are there? Where are they located? How far are they from where you will be staying?

How will your meals be provided? What kinds of restaurants are in the proximity?

What kind of local transportation is available to get around? How will you get from the bus/train station or airport to your accommodations? How will you get to the various sites you wish to visit?

What activities are available to learn about the local culture?

Do you need any special identification or visa to enter this location?

Are there any travel warnings or safety precautions posted by the U.S. State Department relating to this destination? Does the Centers for Disease Control recommend any immunizations or other health precautions for travelers to this destination?

Trip budget:

Transportation to get there:	$ _____
Accommodations:	$ _____
Meals:	$ _____
Entertainment:	$ _____
Cultural activities:	$ _____
Local transportation:	$ _____
Personal expenses:	$ _____
Total Estimated Budget:	$ _____

Personal notes:

A map of my host city/town (affix here):

A map of my host country (affix here):

Appendix 8

Journal Pages

Date: _____

CROSS-CULTURAL OBSERVATIONS:

_____

_____

_____

LANGUAGE LEARNING:

New vocabulary:

_____

_____

Grammar goals/accomplishments:

_____

_____

_____

Comprehension challenges/successes:

_____

_____

_____

What did you do today that contributed to your personal goals?

_____

_____

What did you do today to contribute to your professional interest project?

_____

_____

PERSONAL NOTES:

_____

_____

_____

_____

Date: _____

CROSS-CULTURAL OBSERVATIONS:

_____

_____

_____

LANGUAGE LEARNING:

New vocabulary:

_____

_____

Grammar goals/accomplishments:

_____

_____

_____

Comprehension challenges/successes:

_____

_____

_____

What did you do today that contributed to your personal goals?

_____

_____

What did you do today to contribute to your professional interest project?

_____

_____

PERSONAL NOTES:

_____

_____

_____

_____

Date: _____

CROSS-CULTURAL OBSERVATIONS:

_____

_____

_____

LANGUAGE LEARNING:

New vocabulary:

_____

_____

Grammar goals/accomplishments:

_____

_____

_____

Comprehension challenges/successes:

_____

_____

_____

What did you do today that contributed to your personal goals?

_____

_____

What did you do today to contribute to your professional interest project?

_____

_____

PERSONAL NOTES:

_____

_____

_____

_____

Date: _____

CROSS-CULTURAL OBSERVATIONS:

_____

_____

_____

LANGUAGE LEARNING:

New vocabulary:

_____

_____

Grammar goals/accomplishments:

_____

_____

_____

Comprehension challenges/successes:

_____

_____

_____

What did you do today that contributed to your personal goals?

_____

_____

What did you do today to contribute to your professional interest project?

_____

_____

PERSONAL NOTES:

_____

_____

_____

_____

Date:_____

CROSS-CULTURAL OBSERVATIONS:

_____

_____

_____

LANGUAGE LEARNING:

New vocabulary:

_____

_____

Grammar goals/accomplishments:

_____

_____

_____

Comprehension challenges/successes:

_____

_____

_____

What did you do today that contributed to your personal goals?

_____

_____

What did you do today to contribute to your professional interest project?

_____

_____

PERSONAL NOTES:

_____

_____

_____

_____

Date: _____
CROSS-CULTURAL OBSERVATIONS:

_____

_____

_____

LANGUAGE LEARNING:

New vocabulary:

_____

_____

Grammar goals/accomplishments:

_____

_____

_____

Comprehension challenges/successes:

_____

_____

_____

What did you do today that contributed to your personal goals?

_____

_____

What did you do today to contribute to your professional interest project?

_____

_____

PERSONAL NOTES:

_____

_____

_____

_____

Date: _____

CROSS-CULTURAL OBSERVATIONS:

_____

_____

_____

LANGUAGE LEARNING:

New vocabulary:

_____

_____

Grammar goals/accomplishments:

_____

_____

_____

Comprehension challenges/successes:

_____

_____

_____

What did you do today that contributed to your personal goals?

_____

_____

What did you do today to contribute to your professional interest project?

_____

_____

PERSONAL NOTES:

_____

_____

_____

_____

Date: _____

CROSS-CULTURAL OBSERVATIONS:

_____

_____

_____

LANGUAGE LEARNING:

New vocabulary:

_____

_____

Grammar goals/accomplishments:

_____

_____

_____

Comprehension challenges/successes:

_____

_____

_____

What did you do today that contributed to your personal goals?

_____

_____

What did you do today to contribute to your professional interest project?

_____

_____

PERSONAL NOTES:

_____

_____

_____

_____

Date: _____

CROSS-CULTURAL OBSERVATIONS:

_____

_____

_____

LANGUAGE LEARNING:

New vocabulary:

_____

_____

Grammar goals/accomplishments:

_____

_____

_____

Comprehension challenges/successes:

_____

_____

_____

What did you do today that contributed to your personal goals?

_____

_____

What did you do today to contribute to your professional interest project?

_____

_____

PERSONAL NOTES:

_____

_____

_____

_____

Date: _____

CROSS-CULTURAL OBSERVATIONS:

_____

_____

_____

LANGUAGE LEARNING:

New vocabulary:

_____

_____

Grammar goals/accomplishments:

_____

_____

_____

Comprehension challenges/successes:

_____

_____

_____

What did you do today that contributed to your personal goals?

_____

_____

What did you do today to contribute to your professional interest project?

_____

_____

PERSONAL NOTES:

_____

_____

_____

_____

Date: _____
CROSS-CULTURAL OBSERVATIONS:

_____

_____

_____

LANGUAGE LEARNING:
New vocabulary:

_____

_____

Grammar goals/accomplishments:

_____

_____

_____

Comprehension challenges/successes:

_____

_____

_____

What did you do today that contributed to your personal goals?

_____

_____

What did you do today to contribute to your professional interest project?

_____

_____

PERSONAL NOTES:

_____

_____

_____

_____

Date: _____
CROSS-CULTURAL OBSERVATIONS:

_____

_____

_____

LANGUAGE LEARNING:
New vocabulary:

_____

_____

Grammar goals/accomplishments:

_____

_____

_____

Comprehension challenges/successes:

_____

_____

_____

What did you do today that contributed to your personal goals?

_____

_____

What did you do today to contribute to your professional interest project?

_____

_____

PERSONAL NOTES:

_____

_____

_____

_____

Date: _____

CROSS-CULTURAL OBSERVATIONS:

_____

_____

_____

LANGUAGE LEARNING:

New vocabulary:

_____

_____

Grammar goals/accomplishments:

_____

_____

_____

Comprehension challenges/successes:

_____

_____

_____

What did you do today that contributed to your personal goals?

_____

_____

What did you do today to contribute to your professional interest project?

_____

_____

PERSONAL NOTES:

_____

_____

_____

_____

Date: _____

CROSS-CULTURAL OBSERVATIONS:

_____

_____

_____

LANGUAGE LEARNING:

New vocabulary:

_____

_____

Grammar goals/accomplishments:

_____

_____

_____

Comprehension challenges/successes:

_____

_____

_____

What did you do today that contributed to your personal goals?

_____

_____

What did you do today to contribute to your professional interest project?

_____

_____

PERSONAL NOTES:

_____

_____

_____

_____

Date: _____

CROSS-CULTURAL OBSERVATIONS:

_____

_____

_____

LANGUAGE LEARNING:

New vocabulary:

_____

_____

Grammar goals/accomplishments:

_____

_____

_____

Comprehension challenges/successes:

_____

_____

_____

What did you do today that contributed to your personal goals?

_____

_____

What did you do today to contribute to your professional interest project?

_____

_____

PERSONAL NOTES:

_____

_____

_____

_____

Date: _____

CROSS-CULTURAL OBSERVATIONS:

_____

_____

_____

LANGUAGE LEARNING:

  New vocabulary:

_____

_____

  Grammar goals/accomplishments:

_____

_____

_____

  Comprehension challenges/successes:

_____

_____

_____

What did you do today that contributed to your personal goals?

_____

_____

What did you do today to contribute to your professional interest project?

_____

_____

PERSONAL NOTES:

_____

_____

_____

_____

Date: _____
CROSS-CULTURAL OBSERVATIONS:

_____

_____

_____

LANGUAGE LEARNING:

New vocabulary:

_____

_____

Grammar goals/accomplishments:

_____

_____

_____

Comprehension challenges/successes:

_____

_____

_____

What did you do today that contributed to your personal goals?

_____

_____

What did you do today to contribute to your professional interest project?

_____

_____

PERSONAL NOTES:

_____

_____

_____

_____

Date: _____

CROSS-CULTURAL OBSERVATIONS:

_____

_____

_____

LANGUAGE LEARNING:

New vocabulary:

_____

_____

Grammar goals/accomplishments:

_____

_____

_____

Comprehension challenges/successes:

_____

_____

_____

What did you do today that contributed to your personal goals?

_____

_____

What did you do today to contribute to your professional interest project?

_____

_____

PERSONAL NOTES:

_____

_____

_____

_____

Date: _____

CROSS-CULTURAL OBSERVATIONS:

_____

_____

_____

LANGUAGE LEARNING:

New vocabulary:

_____

_____

Grammar goals/accomplishments:

_____

_____

_____

Comprehension challenges/successes:

_____

_____

_____

What did you do today that contributed to your personal goals?

_____

_____

What did you do today to contribute to your professional interest project?

_____

_____

PERSONAL NOTES:

_____

_____

_____

_____

Date: _____
CROSS-CULTURAL OBSERVATIONS:

_____

_____

_____

LANGUAGE LEARNING:
New vocabulary:

_____

_____

Grammar goals/accomplishments:

_____

_____

_____

Comprehension challenges/successes:

_____

_____

_____

What did you do today that contributed to your personal goals?

_____

_____

What did you do today to contribute to your professional interest project?

_____

_____

PERSONAL NOTES:

_____

_____

_____

_____

Date: _____

CROSS-CULTURAL OBSERVATIONS:

_____

_____

_____

LANGUAGE LEARNING:

New vocabulary:

_____

_____

Grammar goals/accomplishments:

_____

_____

_____

Comprehension challenges/successes:

_____

_____

_____

What did you do today that contributed to your personal goals?

_____

_____

What did you do today to contribute to your professional interest project?

_____

_____

PERSONAL NOTES:

_____

_____

_____

_____

Date: _____

CROSS-CULTURAL OBSERVATIONS:

_____

_____

_____

LANGUAGE LEARNING:

New vocabulary:

_____

_____

Grammar goals/accomplishments:

_____

_____

_____

Comprehension challenges/successes:

_____

_____

_____

What did you do today that contributed to your personal goals?

_____

_____

What did you do today to contribute to your professional interest project?

_____

_____

PERSONAL NOTES:

_____

_____

_____

_____

Date: _____

CROSS-CULTURAL OBSERVATIONS:

_____

_____

_____

LANGUAGE LEARNING:

New vocabulary:

_____

_____

Grammar goals/accomplishments:

_____

_____

_____

Comprehension challenges/successes:

_____

_____

_____

What did you do today that contributed to your personal goals?

_____

_____

What did you do today to contribute to your professional interest project?

_____

_____

PERSONAL NOTES:

_____

_____

_____

_____

Date: _____

CROSS-CULTURAL OBSERVATIONS:

_____

_____

_____

LANGUAGE LEARNING:

New vocabulary:

_____

_____

Grammar goals/accomplishments:

_____

_____

_____

Comprehension challenges/successes:

_____

_____

_____

What did you do today that contributed to your personal goals?

_____

_____

What did you do today to contribute to your professional interest project?

_____

_____

PERSONAL NOTES:

_____

_____

_____

_____

Date: _____

CROSS-CULTURAL OBSERVATIONS:

_____

_____

_____

LANGUAGE LEARNING:

New vocabulary:

_____

_____

Grammar goals/accomplishments:

_____

_____

_____

Comprehension challenges/successes:

_____

_____

_____

What did you do today that contributed to your personal goals?

_____

_____

What did you do today to contribute to your professional interest project?

_____

_____

PERSONAL NOTES:

_____

_____

_____

_____

Date: _____

CROSS-CULTURAL OBSERVATIONS:

_____

_____

_____

LANGUAGE LEARNING:

New vocabulary:

_____

_____

Grammar goals/accomplishments:

_____

_____

_____

Comprehension challenges/successes:

_____

_____

_____

What did you do today that contributed to your personal goals?

_____

_____

What did you do today to contribute to your professional interest project?

_____

_____

PERSONAL NOTES:

_____

_____

_____

_____

Date: _____

CROSS-CULTURAL OBSERVATIONS:

_____

_____

_____

LANGUAGE LEARNING:

New vocabulary:

_____

_____

Grammar goals/accomplishments:

_____

_____

_____

Comprehension challenges/successes:

_____

_____

_____

What did you do today that contributed to your personal goals?

_____

_____

What did you do today to contribute to your professional interest project?

_____

_____

PERSONAL NOTES:

_____

_____

_____

_____

Date: _____

CROSS-CULTURAL OBSERVATIONS:

_____

_____

_____

LANGUAGE LEARNING:

New vocabulary:

_____

_____

Grammar goals/accomplishments:

_____

_____

_____

Comprehension challenges/successes:

_____

_____

_____

What did you do today that contributed to your personal goals?

_____

_____

What did you do today to contribute to your professional interest project?

_____

_____

PERSONAL NOTES:

_____

_____

_____

_____

Date: _____

CROSS-CULTURAL OBSERVATIONS:

_____

_____

_____

LANGUAGE LEARNING:

New vocabulary:

_____

_____

Grammar goals/accomplishments:

_____

_____

_____

Comprehension challenges/successes:

_____

_____

_____

What did you do today that contributed to your personal goals?

_____

_____

What did you do today to contribute to your professional interest project?

_____

_____

PERSONAL NOTES:

_____

_____

_____

_____

Date: _____
CROSS-CULTURAL OBSERVATIONS:

_____

_____

_____

LANGUAGE LEARNING:
New vocabulary:

_____

_____

Grammar goals/accomplishments:

_____

_____

_____

Comprehension challenges/successes:

_____

_____

_____

What did you do today that contributed to your personal goals?

_____

_____

What did you do today to contribute to your professional interest project?

_____

_____

PERSONAL NOTES:

_____

_____

_____

_____

Date: _____
CROSS-CULTURAL OBSERVATIONS:

_____

_____

_____

LANGUAGE LEARNING:
   New vocabulary:

_____

_____

   Grammar goals/accomplishments:

_____

_____

_____

   Comprehension challenges/successes:

_____

_____

_____

What did you do today that contributed to your personal goals?

_____

_____

What did you do today to contribute to your professional interest project?

_____

_____

PERSONAL NOTES:

_____

_____

_____

_____

Date: _____

CROSS-CULTURAL OBSERVATIONS:

_____

_____

_____

LANGUAGE LEARNING:

New vocabulary:

_____

_____

Grammar goals/accomplishments:

_____

_____

_____

Comprehension challenges/successes:

_____

_____

_____

What did you do today that contributed to your personal goals?

_____

_____

What did you do today to contribute to your professional interest project?

_____

_____

PERSONAL NOTES:

_____

_____

_____

_____